ABANDONED STATIONS ON LONDON'S UNDERGROUND

A Photographic Record

J.E. Connor

Preface

This is the second edition of this book which was published in 2000 as a companion to the earlier volume *London's Disused Underground Stations*.

    I have used current line titles to assist the reader in identifying present day remains, although some historical anomalies have occurred. Of particular note is the route to Hounslow, which was worked from the outset by the Metropolitan District Railway, and continued to be part of the District Line until 1964. As it is now only served by the Piccadilly Line, it appears under that heading. This means that the short branch to Hounslow Town, closed in 1909, would be completely isolated if correctly shown as 'District', so it is featured in the Piccadilly section.

    I have included lines outside the bounds of Greater London, such as the Brill branch, together with routes associated with London Transport but not actually part of the Underground system. These include the Docklands Light Railway, and the station at Uxbridge Road, which until 1940 was served by Metropolitan trains linking Edgware Road with what is now Kensington Olympia. I have also featured the experimental pneumatic tube railway which was built in the Crystal Palace grounds during 1864, the Tower Subway and, in response to a suggestion made by many readers of the first edition, the Kingsway Tram Subway.

    At the time of writing various new developments are taking place around the London railway network, including changes to the East London Line which closed to LUL services in December 2007 but is due to reopen as part of the 'Overground' in 2010. Although it is appreciated that the stations have certainly not been abandoned, they will no longer be used by Underground trains, so both this route and the Northern City Line have been included under 'Lost Services'.

    I have featured stations which have been totally closed, together with those where the platforms have been relocated on completely new sites, not overlapping the originals. I have intentionally avoided rebuildings such as West Hampstead and Northwood, where platforms have been moved laterally in connection with track alterations, and also instances of street level buildings being discarded in favour of newer entrances, as at Euston and Green Park.

I would like to stress that all recent photographs of stations in their disused condition were taken with permission and under official supervision.

Photograph credits

I. Baker : 96 (lower).

T Baker : 90 (lower).

H.C. Casserley: 102.

N. Catford: Title page, 8 (all), 41, 44 (upper), 62 (lower), 65 (upper), 70 (both), 71 (all), 72 (lower), 73 (both), 74 (upper and centre), 76 (both) and 77 (upper).

C.D. Connor : 4 (all), 12 (centre and lower), 36 (lower), 62 (upper and centre), 68 (all), 77 (centre and lower, left and right) and back cover lower left.

J.E. Connor : Front cover (all), 9 (lower), 12 (upper),14, 15 (both), 18 (lower), 20, 21 (both), 23 (lower), 28 (all), 29 (both), 30 (both), 31 (centre and lower), 32 (all), 33, 34 (both), 35 (upper), 36 (upper and centre), 43 (lower), 46 (all), 47 (both), 52 (upper), 53 (lower), 54, 55 (all), 56 (upper), 61, 63, 64 (all), 65 (lower), 67 (upper), 69 (both), 72 (upper), 74 (lower), 75 (both), 79 (lower), 84 (both), 87, 88, 89, 90 (upper), 93 (upper and lower), 95 (all), 96 (upper), 97 (lower), 100 (centre),103 (lower),104 (upper) and back cover (right and upper left).

J.E. Connor Collection : 11 (lower), 22, 23 (upper), 25 (upper), 27 (centre and lower), 37, 40 (upper) 43 (centre), 49 (upper), 50, 66, 78, 91 and 97(upper).

A.B. Cross : 103 (upper).

M. Durell Collection : 49 (centre and lower), 59 (both) and 94 (both).

J. C. Gillham : 35 (lower).

G.W. Goslin Collection : 81 (both).

Harrow Library/ G. Kerley collection : 39, 42, 46 (upper), 48, 52 (centre), 53 (upper) and 56 (lower).

D. Hibbert : 44 (lower)

P. Laming Collection : 11 (upper) and 45.

B. Le Jeune : 104 (centre and lower).

Lens of Sutton Association : 16, 17 (both), 18 (upper), 40 (lower), 82 and 93 (centre).

Locomotive Club of Great Britain /Ken Nunn Collection : 31 (upper) and 86 (lower).

London & North Eastern Railway : 13.

London Transport Museum : 6 (both), 7 (both), 19, 24, 25 (lower). 26, 27 (upper), 38, 43 (upper), 52 (lower), 79 (upper), 83 and 86 (upper).

D. Rose : 60 (all).

Southern Railway : 85 (upper),.

M. Thomson collection : 67 (lower).

W. Watters : 9 (upper).

W. Watters Collection : 58.

Line engravings from contemporary publications etc : 57, 99, 100 (upper and lower) and 101. .

ISBN 978 0 947699 41 4
First published 2000.
Second Edition revised and enlarged 2008.
Published by Connor & Butler Ltd.,
PO Box 9561, Colchester, Essex CO1 9DL.
Printed by Mid-Essex Printers (01206) 572662.
© J.E, Connor 2008.

Contents

Maps

Index

All stations are included under the names which they carried at time of closure. These are shown in this index in capital letters, whilst alternative names appear in upper and lower case. Those shown within quotation marks and italicised were proposed but never carried.

Introduction

The closed stations on London's Underground are many and varied. Some lie hidden away behind walls on deep level tube lines, whilst others can be easily seen. As the years progress, a number have passed beyond living memory, and it may be hard to imagine that each of them was once a familiar feature to past generations of Londoners.

Occasionally it is possible to glimpse these old stations from passing trains, although it takes a very experienced eye to recognise some of them. Nevertheless, a few remain obvious, and the imaginative traveller can easily conjure up thoughts of ghosts lurking in the dark cross passages.

It is perhaps this air of mystery which adds to their interest. After all, there are numerous disused station sites on the main line suburban routes around London, but somehow, these do not seem to exude the same atmosphere as one which lies seemingly forgotten in the gloom of a tunnel.

A few abandoned Underground stations were put to good use during the Second World War, when they were converted into air raid shelters, whilst a couple on the Piccadilly Line were adapted for government purposes. Even today, ephemeral relics such as faded paper signs pointing to long gone wartime first aid posts still cling to walls, and although passed by millions of passengers daily, these remain largely unseen.

This book takes a look at the various forgotten stations on the Underground system, and tells of when they were built, why they were closed, and what, if anything, still survives of them.

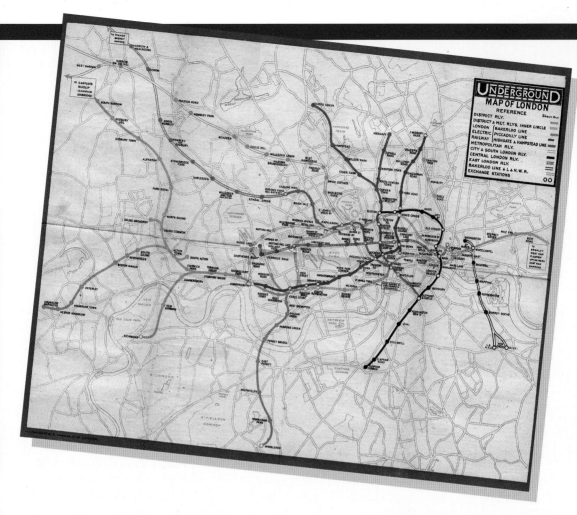

The Underground network has undergone drastic expansion and numerous changes since this map was published in October 1919.

At this time, the Piccadilly Line only linked Hammersmith with Finsbury Park whilst what is now the Northern Line had yet to be extended to serve Morden, Edgware, Mill Hill East and High Barnet as it does today.

The Central Line was restricted to the route between Liverpool Street and Wood Lane, whilst both the Victoria and Jubilee Lines were still very much in the future.

Stations shown on this map which have since completely closed are:
Aldwych
British Museum
Brompton Road
City Road
Down Street
Marlborough Road
St. Johns Wood Road
St. Mary's
Shoreditch
South Acton
South Kentish Town
Swiss Cottage
Uxbridge Road
Wood Lane
York Road
Some have also been subject to resiting or renaming.

Wood Lane

In order to serve the Franco-British Exhibition, the Central London Railway decided to build a new station near its existing depot at Wood Lane. The route was extended from the former terminus Shepherds Bush, and reached the new premises by way of a sharply-curved single track loop.

The station was brought into use on 14th May 1908, to coincide with the opening of the exhibition, and had its entrance on the east side of Wood Lane.

The street level building was designed by Harry Bell Measures, and stood partly beneath an ornate overhead walkway which linked the exhibition grounds with Uxbridge Road. In this view, the CLR power station, with the word 'Tube' displayed on its chimney can be seen in the background.

On arrival at Wood Lane, passengers originally alighted at platform one, which is seen beyond the track, then made their way to the exhibition by means of the footbridge. Those travelling towards central London joined their train from platform two, on which the photographer was standing when this view was taken in 1935.

The street level building was reconstructed under the direction of Stanley Heaps around 1915, two years after the CLR became part of the Underground Group.

An idiosyncracy of Wood Lane station was this section of movable platform, added to the east end of No 1 in 1928. Its existence allowed longer trains to be operated, as when the depot needed to be accessed, it could be swung clear of the points by the signalman in the adjoining cabin.

A 68187

Central London Railway.
Issued subject to the Coy. Bye-laws and Stations.
WOOD LANE 4
WOOD LANE 4
(4 TO 4)
TOTTENHAM CT. RD.
TOTTENHAM CT. RD.   TOTTENHAM CT. RD.
Fare 2d.   Fare 2d.
Available on day of issue only.

When the Central London Line was extended to Ealing Broadway in 1920, two sub-surface platforms were added to Wood Lane. Because the station still had to be reached by way of the old single track loop however, it was not ideal, so eventually replacement premises were opened at White City on 23rd November 1947, and Wood Lane was closed. Both sub-surface platforms survived more or less intact for many years and even retained some of their nameboards along with a few tattered posters.

Until 18th July 1948, passenger trains continued to pass through both the abandoned sub-surface platforms at Wood Lane. After this however a new westbound tunnel was completed and the line through the erstwhile platform 4, seen here, was converted into a depot approach.

After closure the premises became derelict, but they retained many of their features, as can be seen from this photograph which looks east across the site in the 1970s. At bottom left is the street level building, with the former concourse area immediately behind. Above this, the remains of the passenger footbridge spans the curving trackbed, with platform 2 on the left and platform 1 to the right. Behind platform 1 stands part of the old CLR power station. The passenger station site was subsequently cleared for redevelopment, with the street level building being demolished in autumn 2003.

This 1970 view was taken from the old concourse and shows the rear of the street frontage on the right and the stairs descending to platform 3 on the left.

British Museum

Soon after the CLR opened, Shurrey's Publications issued a series of postcards featuring cartoon characters at each of the stations. Generally the names were shown correctly, but in the case of British Museum, an abbreviated form was used, presumably for humorous reasons, as seen below.

British Museum station was opened by the Central London Railway on 30th July 1900, and had its entrance at the corner of High Holborn and Bloomsbury Court.

After the opening of the nearby Great Northern Piccadilly & Brompton Railway station at Holborn, passengers began using this as an interchange with British Museum, but the facilities were less than perfect, and meant walking between the two at street level.

A plan to build new Central London Line platforms at Holborn was authorised in 1914, but the scheme failed to materialise due to the intervention of the First World War.

It was later revived however, and the new station was brought into use on 25th September 1933, when British Museum closed.

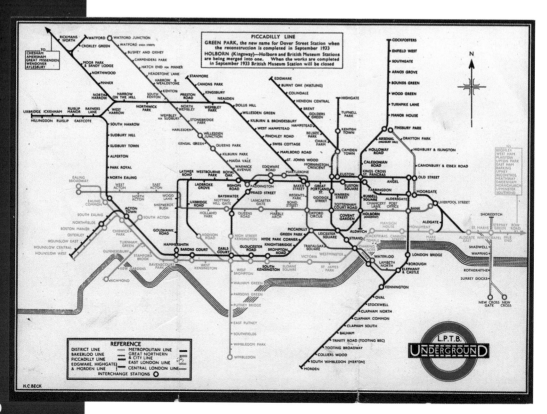

This is British Museum soon after opening, with the white tiled walls and wooden platforms, which were featured at all original CLR stations. The latter became regarded as a potential fire hazard, and were therefore rebuilt in concrete, with those at British Museum being replaced towards the end of 1909. The publisher of the original postcard obviously appreciated the value of advertising!

Here we see the station in its later days. Although the print is undated the photograph is thought to have been taken shortly before closure.

The street level building, designed by Harry Bell Measures, is seen above as it appeared in 1968, twenty-one years before demolition. It was originally constructed with a flat roof, but this was only intended as a temporary arrangement, as office accommodation was erected above it around 1902.

During the Second World War, the former platform tunnels were converted into air raid shelters, and these were brought into use in September 1941. Surprisingly reminders of this period were still evident in the 1990s.

The shelter accommodation was located on two levels, with the upper floor constructed of concrete. After hostilities ended, the additional floors, along with walls which separated shelterers from passing trains were removed, leaving just the platform-tunnels which can still be seen from a passing train.

Loughton

The original station at Loughton stood to the east of the High Road and was the terminus of the Eastern Counties Railway branch from Stratford. No photographs are known to exist, but it is understood to have comprised two platforms, with the principal building, probably wooden, located on the down side. It opened on 22nd August 1856, but closed in April 1865, when the branch was extended to Ongar. As it was deemed impractical to continue the tracks beyond their original alignment, the extension diverged south of the old terminus and was provided with a completely new two-platform station. The approach to its predecessor was then developed as a goods yard and carriage sidings, although the terminus itself was abandoned.

The 1865 station was subject to various alterations and improvements during its existence, but retained its original main building, which again stood on the down side. For many years Loughton was a popular destination for excursionists visiting Epping Forest and it is understood that a platform was constructed on the west side of the carriage sidings around the 1870s to handle some of the additional traffic. This was accessed from the road by way of a brick building and in later times this was misleadingly referred to locally as *"The Old Station"*.

As part of the plan to extend Central Line services over the route, the London & North Eastern Railway constructed the present Loughton station a little to the east of its 1865 predecessor and brought it into use on 28th April 1940.

This view, taken in the 1930s, shows the up platform of the second Loughton station, looking towards Epping and Ongar. The present premises are located approximately 200-300yds to the north-east, around where the tracks are seen curving off into the distance.

GREAT EASTERN RAILWAY
Not transferable Issued subject to Regulations
in the Company's Time Tables
LOUGHTON to
Loughton   Loughton
GEORGE LANE
George Lane   George Lane
5d   FARE   5d
Second Class
Available on day of issue only

Epping-Ongar

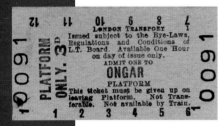

The line linking Loughton and Epping with Ongar was opened by the Great Eastern Railway on 24th April 1865.

Under a pre-Second World War plan, the Central Line was to extend eastwards from its existing terminus at Liverpool Street, and ultimately travel through to Ongar. The branch first appeared on Underground maps in 1938, but work was delayed by the outbreak of hostilities the following year, and the route was not officially absorbed by London Transport until 25th September 1949.

In the meantime, tube services were extended to Woodford in 1947, and eventually reached Epping two years later. However, the remainder of the branch was destined to retain a shuttle service of steam trains until 18th November 1957, when electrification to Ongar was finally completed.

Unfortunately, the single track section between Epping and Ongar served a lightly populated area, and by 1970 was losing around £100,000 a year. This led to it being proposed for closure, but although the branch survived, its existence remained under threat, and services subsequently became restricted to peak hours only.

Eventually the inevitable happened, and closure came after traffic on Friday 30th September 1994.

The route was subsequently the subject of preservation proposals and the Epping Ongar Volunteer Railway commenced operating return trips between Ongar and North Weald on Sundays and Bank Holidays from 3rd October 2005 using a diesel multiple unit.

North Weald was provided with a passing loop and additional platform from 14th August 1949, but the expected increase in traffic never materialised, so it was closed from 18th October 1976, leaving just the original platform in use. Here we see the 1865 station building as it appeared in 1969.

Blake Hall had the unenviable reputation of being the least used station on the LT system, and closed after traffic on 31st October 1981. The 1865 building, which is seen here, subsequently became a Grade II listed structure and is now a private house. Both photographs on this page date from 1969.

The terminus at Ongar comprised a single platform, and in steam days boasted a single-road engine shed of 1865 vintage. Freight traffic was handled in the station goods yard until 18th April 1966, and the signal box, just visible in the distance, was abolished three years later.

South Acton

On 15th May 1899, a 1,232 yard single line spur was opened for freight traffic between the Metropolitan District Railway at Mill Hill Park (now Acton Town) and South Acton on the North & South Western Junction Railway.

Six years later the track was doubled, and electrified. A single platform station was constructed at South Acton, and a passenger service commenced on 13th June 1905.

At first, passenger trains operated between South Acton and Hounslow Barracks, but in time destinations also included South Harrow and Uxbridge.

The line joined the NSWJR at District Junction, a little beyond South Acton station, but the connection was only intended for freight traffic. When this ceased, the junction was no longer required, so it was severed in 1930, and two years later the second track was lifted.

From 15th February 1932, through workings from other parts of the MDR were withdrawn, and the South Acton branch was reduced to a shuttle which ran back and forth to a bay platform at Acton Town.

The MDR terminus adjoined the up side of South Acton station on the North & South Western Junction Railway (now part of the North London Line), but was at a slightly higher level, as seen to the right of this view which dates from the late 1950s.

In the late 1930s, a pair of 1923 G Stock cars were converted so that they could be driven from either end. In this form they became resident on the Acton Town - South Acton shuttle, and can be seen here at the branch terminus in the 1950s.

Throughout much of the day, the service operated at ten minute intervals, and the journey time was so quick that it was thought the crew could do an out and back trip from Acton Town by the time the messroom kettle boiled. This gave rise to the turn being known by staff as 'The Tea Run', although the origin of its other nickname, 'The Pony', is rather more obscure.

Eventually however, LT announced that this unremunerative, if characterful service would cease, and trains were withdrawn after traffic on 28th February 1959. Official closure followed on 2nd March.

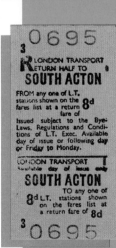

The track was lifted within a few months of closure, leaving the abandoned station to stand for a short while before it was completely demolished.

SOUTH ACTON UNDERGROUND BRANCH LINE IS NOW CLOSED

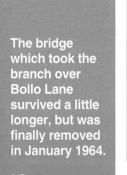

The bridge which took the branch over Bollo Lane survived a little longer, but was finally removed in January 1964.

Earl's Court

The original station of this name, which stood on the east side of Earl's Court Road, opened on 30th October 1871 and consisted of two platforms, of which one was an island.

Initially there was little local development, as the surrounding area was largely given over to market gardening. Therefore, the station only required to be a very modest affair, with a wooden street level building.

This was badly damaged by fire on 30th December 1875, and although subsequently repaired, the decision was made to resite the premises to the opposite side of Earl's Court Road.

The replacement station opened on 1st February 1878, when its predecessor was closed, and soon demolished.

Staff pose with 4-4-0T locomotive No 4 at the City end of the original Earl's Court station in May 1876. The gentleman on the platform wearing a top hat is Mr T.S. Speck, the Metropolitan District Railway's Locomotive Superintendent and Resident Engineer.

Tower Hill

The original Tower Hill station was opened as Mark Lane on 6th October 1884, and had its entrance at the corner of Byward Street and Seething Lane.

Its street level building was replaced by a new booking hall incorporated into an office block in 1911, but apart from this, the station's only major change came on 1st September 1946, when it was renamed Tower Hill.

In time, the station proved to be inadequate, and as there was no room for expansion on its existing site, authority was received to relocate the premises further east.

The site chosen was that previously occupied by the short lived Metropolitan Railway station at Tower of London *(See pp 22-23)*, and the building contract was let in November 1964.

The present Tower Hill station opened on 5th February 1967, as a direct replacement for its predecessor which closed the same day.

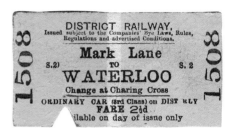

The westbound platform, as it appeared on 28th March 1966.

The seemingly deserted eastbound platform at Tower Hill in February 1967, shortly before the station was closed. Although the westbound side was subsequently demolished to facilitate track alterations, the platform seen here still exists, and can be glimpsed from a passing train, immediately west of the present Tower Hill.

A 1966 view of the street level entrance, as incorporated into an office block fifty-five years earlier. The lettering above the arched opening to the right read 'Mark Lane Station Buildings', but although the building still survives, this has long-since disappeared.

The Tower of London

This short lived station owed its origins to inter-company squabbling between the Metropolitan and Metropolitan District Railways regarding the completion of the Inner Circle, or Circle Line as it is now known.

The project was a joint venture between the two, but having suffered from lack of finance, the MDR section got as far east as Mansion House then stopped.

The Metropolitan however wanted to press on, and eventually built as much of the route as the authorising Parliamentary Act allowed. They finally reached Trinity Square, and on 25th September 1882 opened a station there which was named The Tower of London.

This 'go it alone' venture engendered more bad feeling between the companies, but eventually the atmosphere improved, and the Inner Circle at last became a reality.

A new station was opened at nearby Mark Lane *(See pp 20-21)* on 6th October 1884, and a week later, on 13th October, The Tower of London closed.

The station was erected in the remarkably short time of two days and three nights. Its street level building stood on the east side of Trinity Square, near the corner with Trinity Place, and is seen here around 1935.

The disused Tower of London station remained largely intact until 1903 when its platforms were removed in connection with electrification work which was then taking place. The street level building survived much longer however, and was not demolished until September 1940, around a month after this photograph was taken. The gaps beside the line where the platforms had been removed remained visible into the 1960s, as did a short section of erstwhile stairway handrail, but with the plan to re-use the site for a new Tower Hill station, all relics of the original premises were swept away.

The contract for building the new Tower Hill station was let to W & C French Ltd in November 1964, and the new premises were brought into use, albeit in an unfinished state on 5th February 1967. Today, millions of passengers use the present Tower Hill without realising that at one time, a station called The Tower of London once stood on the same site, even if its useful life was restricted to just two years!

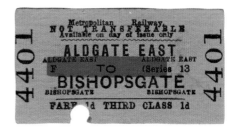

Aldgate East

To the west of the present Aldgate East lies the site of the first station to carry this name.

It was opened by the Metropolitan and Metropolitan District Railways on 6th October 1884, and stood on the north side of Whitechapel High Street.

So that longer trains could be accommodated between the junctions west of the station, a resiting scheme was devised.

The work of building the new station was carried out with only a minimum disruption to traffic, and the premises were brought into use on 31st October 1938, the same day that the original closed.

The street level building in its original form, prior to being reconstructed in 1914 under the direction of Harry Wharton Ford.

This view, taken from a vintage commercial postcard, shows Harry Wharton Ford's street level building to the right. Although this became derelict after closure, it remained standing into the 1950s when it was demolished for redevelopment.

The realigned junction at Aldgate East would occupy part of the original station site, so the platforms were rebuilt in wood to make them easier to remove when the time came. The resiting project was a major engineering feat, but the only time the line needed to close was on the day of the changeover. This view shows the old station whilst work was underway.

St. Mary's (Whitechapel Road.)

St. Mary's (Whitechapel) station opened on 3rd March 1884, and was used initially by South Eastern Railway trains from Addiscombe Road, which travelled by way of a spur off the East London Line, known as 'The St. Mary's Curve'. These were withdrawn seven months later from 1st October 1884, a week before full Metropolitan & District services were introduced over the lines east of Bishopsgate and Mansion House.

The station was renamed St. Mary's (Whitechapel Road) on 26th January 1923.

Metropolitan & District R'ys.
NOT TRANSFERABLE
Available on day of issue only.
ST.MARY'S (WHITECHAPEL)
ST. MARY'S W'chapel   ST. MARY'S W'chapel
G   Series 63.
TO
DEPTFORD RD. For South-wark Park
Deptford Rd for S. Park   Deptford Rd for S. Park
Via Shadwell
FARE 2d THIRD CLASS 2d
1890 ... 1890

Metropolitan Railway.
Available on day of issue only.
Issued subject to the Co's Bye-Laws & Regulations
St. Mary's Whitechapel
ST. MARY'S(W'CHAPEL)   ST. MARY'S(W'CHAPEL)
TO
LIVERPOOL ST.
LIVERPOOL ST   LIVERPOOL ST
VIA ALDGATE EAST
FARE 1d. THIRD CLASS 1d.
3364 ... 3364

London Passenger Transport Board.
Issued subject to the Bye-Laws, Regulations and advertised Conditions of the Board.
CHILD
St. Marys (Whitechapel 1) to
BROMLEY (L.M.S)
Via Mile End
or intermediately.
- 2d THIRD CLASS FARE **2d -**
Available day of issue only.
076 ... 076

The station's street level building stood on the south side of Whitechapel Road and, apart from some minor alterations, remained largely unaltered throughout its existence. This view dates from around the First World War and shows it before the erection of the adjoining Rivoli cinema which opened in 1921.

FAST ELECTRIC TRAINS FROM THIS STATION TO

MANSION HOUSE		LIVERPOOL STREET
BLACKFRIARS	SHADWELL	FINSBURY PARK
CHARING CROSS	WAPPING	EUSTON SQUARE
VICTORIA	ROTHERHITHE	KINGS CROSS
WATERLOO	SURREY DOCKS	PADDINGTON
EARLS COURT	NEW CROSS	SHEPHERDS BUSH
WALHAM GREEN		HAMMERSMITH

ST MARYS (WHITECHAPEL ROAD) STATION

The station's exterior nameboard was changed to one which displayed its post-1923 title, but tickets appear to have carried the earlier name to the end. This view dates from the 1930s.

The 1921 Rivoli cinema dwarfed the station's street level building, as is apparent from the photograph on the right.

STATION PERMANENTLY CLOSED
NEAREST STATIONS
WHITECHAPEL ← → ALDGATE EAST

St. Mary's closed from 1st May 1938, almost six months prior to the resited Aldgate East station being opened nearby. This view shows the street level building immediately after closure, with a large board directing potential passengers to Whitechapel or Aldgate East, which were the stations on either side. The disused platforms were later adapted to serve as an air raid shelter during the Second World War. However, the former street level building was badly damaged by a bomb on 22nd October 1940 and had to be demolished, so a new shelter entrance had to be provided. The same raid brought an end to the Rivoli cinema, although part of its battered remains survived into the early 1960s.

The work of converting St. Mary's into a air-raid shelter continued, even though the replacement entrance was itself destroyed before completion. Parts of the former shelter accommodation still survive but these are hidden behind brick walls erected at the time and are therefore not visible from passing trains. This view looks west and shows the former eastbound platform as it appeared on 25th January 1996 along with the remains of the old footbridge.

In addition to some of the erstwhile shelter facilities, a number of the station's original features survive at track level, although once again these are largely hidden from passing trains by walls erected during the Second World War. To the left we see part of the stairway which once served the westbound platform, whilst below are a pair of roof columns with Egyptianesque lotus capitals, similar to those visible in the view of Aldgate East reproduced on page 25.

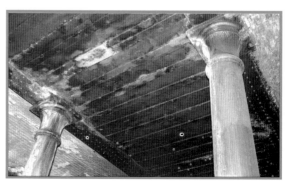

Mudchute

Until 1999, the Docklands Light Railway route which now serves Lewisham, terminated on the north bank of the Thames at Island Gardens. The final stretch of line, south of Crossharbour utilised the surviving formation of the old Millwall Extension Railway, which opened in 1871-2, and closed in 1926. Between Crossharbour and Island Gardens stood the station at Mudchute, which was located on a new section of concrete viaduct, and opened to the public with the initial section of DLR on 31st August 1987.

As it was not possible to extend the line south of the existing terminus, the route to Lewisham needed to branch off near Crossharbour, then dive into cutting, and eventually tunnel to pass under the Thames. This resulted in the earlier formation being abandoned, and the closure of the original stations at Mudchute and Island Gardens in January 1999.

The DLR was officially opened by HM The Queen on 30th July 1987, but public services did not commence for another month. The view above records the platforms at Mudchute under construction on 7th June 1986, whilst that below shows P86 vehicle No 07 entering the station on 31st August 1987, heading towards Island Gardens.

The platform canopies at the original Mudchute station were typical of those provided on the initial sections of the DLR which opened in 1987. This view looks towards Crossharbour and was taken just prior to closure.

After closure, very little time elapsed before Mudchute station was demolished. On Friday 15th January 1999, the lamps and signs were removed, with the track being lifted soon after. The following week, the towers which housed the lifts were knocked down, and by the end of the month virtually everything had disappeared. The new Mudchute station is located in cutting, on a site east of its predecessor, and opened on Saturday 20th November 1999.

Island Gardens

The terminus at Island Gardens occupied part of the site once used by the former Millwall Extension Railway station at North Greenwich & Cubitt Town, which had opened in 1872 and closed in 1926. The MER had diverged from the London & Blackwall Railway at Millwall Junction, then continued to 'North Greenwich' by way of intermediate stations at South Dock and Millwall Docks. The old terminus remained standing for forty-three years after closure, but was eventually demolished to make way for a rowing club building. With the advent of the DLR, the rest of the site was cleared, and a new viaduct was erected to accommodate Island Gardens. Although built largely of concrete, this was faced with bricks, and the resulting arches were fitted out as shop units.

Millwall Extension Railway locomotive No 4 stands at North Greenwich after arriving with the branch train from Millwall Junction on 14th September 1910.

Because it used the old Millwall Extension Railway viaduct on its approach to Island Gardens, this section of the DLR was restricted to a single track. At the terminus however, it splayed out to serve two platforms, separated by a distinctive glass dome which accommodated lifts and a stairway. The photographs seen here were taken on 31st August 1987.

Vehicle No 39 is seen at Island Gardens in the small hours of Saturday 9th January 1999, having just arrived from Poplar. It subsequently departed from platform 2 at around 01.09 for the final run over the historic Millwall Extension Railway viaduct.

Left : Shortly before midnight on Friday 8th January a sign was placed on the wall beneath platform 1, although it was temporarily covered with brown paper whilst the service remained in operation. The plaque above commemorated the Royal Opening of the DLR by HM The Queen on 30th July 1987.

Below : The old Millwall Extension Railway viaduct north of the station carried the DLR above Millwall Park. This 682 yard structure was the only notable piece of civil engineering on the former MER, and is now disused for the second time in its existence. This view looks across from the park entrance and was taken in 1968.

Shoreditch

Shoreditch station was opened with the East London Railway extension linking Wapping with the Great Eastern at Liverpool Street on 10th April 1876. Its two platforms were located 9chains east of the junction with the GER and were accessed from a single storey building on the north side of Pedley Street.

Passenger services were initially provided by the London Brighton & South Coast Railway, which operated to and from Liverpool Street, but these were cut back to terminate at Shoreditch from 1st January 1886. In connection with this, the track layout was altered so that locomotives could run round their stock, but the station was still being used by through trains, as the Great Eastern had commenced operating services between Liverpool Street and destinations south of the Thames Tunnel.

All local steam passenger services ceased when public electric working commenced on 31st March 1913, although freights continued to pass through, as did some excursion trains.

The electric services were provided by the Metropolitan Railway until 1933 when they were taken over by the LPTB, but it was not until 1949 that the East London Line officially became part of London Transport.

For many years Shoreditch station had restricted opening hours and was latterly only served during Monday-Friday peak periods and for a few hours on Sundays.

By the mid-1960s the East London Line was being operated by trains of Q Stock, as seen in this photograph of Shoreditch station taken in 1967. The old down platform, visible to the right, had been little used since electrification and was officially closed in 1928. It retained its awning and stairway at least until the second half of the next decade, but these had long-gone by the time this photograph was taken. The viaduct above the formation served the old GER Bishopsgate goods depot which closed following a fire in 1964.

Freight trains using the connection with the former GER ceased to operate in the 1960s and the junction was removed on 17th April 1966, when buffer stops were erected at the west end of the station. The old down line was lifted soon after, although double-track running continued east of the platforms. This view, dating from 1969, looks down from the disused Bishopsgate viaduct and shows the points leading to the second track in the distance.

Apart from a few minor changes, the surviving platform remained little altered throughout its existence. Here it is seen in 1969, looking towards Whitechapel.

Although located in Pedley Street, the station entrance was only a short distance from Brick Lane, to which it was linked by the passageway seen on the left. It seems that the name 'Brick Lane' had once been considered for the station, but this was dropped in favour of Shoreditch prior to opening. The photograph reproduced here dates from the 1980s and was taken on a Sunday morning, when the station was open to serve nearby street markets.

EAST LONDON RAILWAY.
Available on the **DATE** of issue **ONLY.**
This Ticket is issued subject to the Regulations
& conditions stated in the Company's Time
Tables & Bills.
SHOREDITCH
No.1 TO
New Cross. nx
3d. THIRD CLASS. 3d.
0330

SHOREDITCH

Until the 1950s, the platform nameboards were of the Metropolitan type, but reputedly because the ELR had once belonged to the Southern Railway, their backing diamonds were green instead of the more familiar red.

When plans were announced to extend the East London Line it became apparent that the existing formation serving Shoreditch could not be utilised so the station had to close. The extension would diverge north of Whitechapel, then climb to the level of the old Bishopsgate viaduct before reaching a replacement station at Shoreditch High Street. From here it would cross the road on a new bridge then join the erstwhile Broad Street route and continue to Dalston Junction. This view looks from the booking hall towards the platform stairs in May 2006 and includes a closure notice by the door.

Closure took place after traffic on Friday 9th June 2006, when a special last train was operated to convey invited guests to Whitechapel. This displayed the legends '1876 ' and '2006' signifying the years of opening and closure and is seen at Shoreditch awaiting departure.

New Cross

The southern terminus of the East London Railway, which opened for public traffic from Wapping on 7th December 1869.

It comprised two platforms, and although it adjoined the eastern side of the existing London Brighton & South Coast Railway station at New Cross, it was at a slightly lower level, and completely separate.

The ELR was extended northwards to a junction with the Great Eastern Railway near Bishopsgate *(See Shoreditch)* in April 1876, and following the introduction of through services between Liverpool Street and Croydon, the earlier terminus closed from 1st November 1876.

With the opening of the Metropolitan and Metropolitan District Joint line towards Whitechapel, both these companies began operating onto the ELR, by way of the new St. Mary's Curve, and the old New Cross terminus once again came into its own. It was reopened on 1st October 1884 for the use of MDR trains, but eventually, after track alterations had been carried out, these were diverted into the adjacent LBSCR station.

Closure came for the second time on 1st September 1886, and the abandoned terminus was eventually demolished fourteen years later.

The former LBSCR station was renamed New Cross Gate on 9th July 1923, and served as one of the southern termini used by the East London Line until Underground operation of the route ceased in December 2007.

Very few photographs appear to exist of the old East London Railway terminus at New Cross, although this is not surprising as it closed so long ago. This view was taken on 18th July 1898 and shows the station around two years before demolition. As can be seen it was still largely intact at the time, although the nameboard had been removed leaving just the empty frame on the left.

Hammersmith

The original terminus of the Hammersmith & City Railway was opened, along with the line from Bishop's Road, Paddington, on 13th June 1864. The route was independently financed, but supported by the Metropolitan and Great Western Railways. It was laid with both standard (4ft 8$\frac{1}{2}$in) and broad gauge (7ft 0$\frac{1}{4}$in) track, as at that time the GWR still used the latter, which had been favoured by its engineer, Isambard Kingdom Brunel.

When opened, the line was served by GWR broad gauge trains which operated at half-hourly intervals between Hammersmith and Farringdon Street. At the beginning of the following month, these were joined by a GWR service which ran to Addison Road (now Kensington Olympia) via Notting Hill (now Ladbroke Grove), but it was not until 1st April 1865 that Metropolitan standard gauge trains made their debut on the route.

From 1st June 1866, the Hammersmith & City came under joint Met & GW management, and was taken over by the two larger companies the following year. An agreement was subsequently reached to remove the broad gauge rail, and from then on all GW services were formed of standard gauge locomotives and stock.

At around the same time, the London & South Western Railway was in the process of building its Kensington to Richmond line *(See Hammersmith Grove Road p.85)*, and in doing so impinged upon the site of the H&CR terminus. Therefore a new station, with standard gauge track only, was opened a few hundred feet to the south on 1st December 1868 and the original was closed.

Metropolitan Railway 4-4-0T No 4 (formerly named *Mercury*) stands at Hammersmith around 1865, with the mixed gauge track in evidence.

Shepherd's Bush

Shepherd's Bush was one of the original intermediate stations on the Hammersmith & City Railway, and opened with the line on 13th June 1864.

Its entrance was sited on the west side of Railway Approach, and was rather awkwardly positioned between two main thoroughfares. From the booking hall, which was positioned within a viaduct arch, stairs ascended to the two wooden platforms above.

The line was electrified in 1906, and various improvements were subsequently planned. Amongst these was the replacement of Shepherd's Bush with new stations on either side. That to the north carried the same name, whilst that to the south became Goldhawk Road.

Both of these were brought into use on 1st April 1914, when the original station closed. The platforms and attendant buildings were demolished in 1915, although the stairways went the previous year, no doubt to deter trespassing. The former booking hall was retained however, and converted into an office to serve the new retail market which opened in Railway Approach on 29th June 1914.

Metropolitan Railway 4-4-0T No 22 is seen at the original Shepherd's Bush Hammersmith & City Line station, as she pauses with a train in the early years of the twentieth century.

White City

Opened as Wood Lane (Exhibition) on 1st May 1908, this station had its entrance at the western end of Macfarlane Place. As its original name implied, it was constructed to serve the Franco-British Exhibition of that year and contemporary Metropolitan Railway publicity boasted it was *"The only station right in the grounds"*.

It was retained after the exhibition closed on 31st October 1908, but within a couple of years traffic began to decline. It was therefore closed from 1st November 1914, but remained intact, and was reopened for one day only on 5th November 1920 as 'Wood Lane (White City)' to serve a motor show. From then on it was opened on an 'as required' basis, mainly in connection with greyhound racing, which was held at White City Stadium.

It was renamed White City on 23rd November 1947, but was last used on 24th October 1959. The following day, one of its platforms was damaged by fire, and the station was permanently closed. It was announced in the spring of 1961 that it was to be demolished and it disappeared soon after.

In 2008 a new station, named 'Wood Lane', was under construction north-east of its former site.

The view above shows the station platforms sometime between 1908 and 1914, whilst that to the left records the exterior at an unknown date, possibly around the time of closure.

Charing Cross

Following an official opening by HRH The Prince of Wales on the previous day, public services on the Jubilee Line between Charing Cross and Stanmore commenced on 1st May 1979.

The route had been planned as The Fleet Line, but its name was changed during construction, in honour of The Queen's Silver Jubilee.

Although the section linking Charing Cross with Baker Street was new, the remainder of the route had recently been part of the Bakerloo Line.

When the Jubilee Line was extended to Stratford however, the new route branched off near Green Park, and the section into Charing Cross closed after traffic on Friday 19th November 1999.

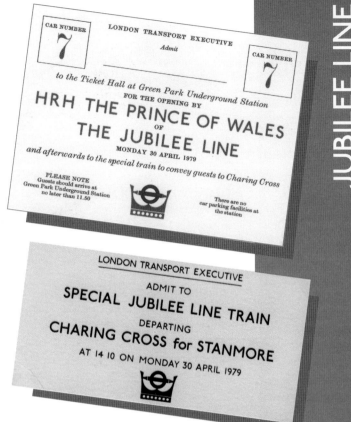

The platform seat recesses featured Nelson-inspired murals designed by David Gentleman, as seen to the right of this view.

Lords

This station was opened as St. John's Wood Road on 13th April 1868, and was one of two intermediate passing places on the otherwise single track Metropolitan & Saint John's Wood Railway. This nominally independent company was absorbed by the larger Metropolitan Railway in 1882, and during the same year, its line was doubled throughout.

The station was extremely busy during the cricket season, due to its proximity to Lord's ground, and in the 1920s was deemed worthy of a substantial rebuild.

A new street level building, designed by architect C.W. Clark was grafted onto the original, whilst a concrete and iron mezzanine floor was erected above the platforms to provide space for some lock-up garages.

The station was officially renamed St. John's Wood from 1st April 1925, and six months later, Clark's new building was completed. Outside the cricket season traffic levels were poor, and the station's opening hours were reduced from 1st October 1929. Its platforms were subsequently lengthened to take eight car trains, but when a plan to extend the Bakerloo Line from Baker Street to Finchley Road was authorised, its days became numbered.

Following a suggestion from the Marylebone Cricket Club, it was renamed Lords on 11th June 1939, but its life under this guise proved very short, as it closed when the Bakerloo Line Extension opened on 20th November the same year, with a new station nearby named St. John's Wood.

It was thought that Lords may have been retained and used during the cricket season, but it was damaged during the Second World War, and its closure proved permanent.

Although not technically perfect, this extremely rare view , taken in the 1930s, shows the station platforms as they appeared in their final years. Although the name had officially been changed to St. John's Wood in 1925, it seems that the platform signs remained unaltered.

The street level building stood on the south side of St. John's Wood Road, close to the junction with Park Road. The photograph above shows it in the 1920s, with a hut outside used as a supplementary ticket office when the station was busy with cricket traffic. The view on the right shows a horse-drawn 'bus ambling by around the dawn of the twentieth century.

C.W. Clark's frontage is seen here as it appeared in 1968, twenty-nine years after the station closed.

Although the station was provided with a new front section in the 1920s, a substantial part of the original street level building survived at the rear as is evident from this photograph which was taken in 1969, when demolition was in its early stages. The site was subsequently redeveloped, but vague traces of the station remain at track level and can be seen from passing trains.

,0001

Ist Cl	LT	
	LORDS	
2d	to	
Issued subject to the Bye-Laws, Regulations and Conditions of the Board. Available day of issue only	Baker Street Swiss Cottage	
	or Intermediately	
2d		

LORDS
'0001

Because it closed so soon after renaming, relics of the station showing the name 'Lords' are extremely rare. However, the upper part of a roundel latterly found its way to a location in the outer suburbs, where its back was used for mixing cement!

Marlborough Road

Marlborough Road station was opened on the Metropolitan & Saint John's Wood Railway on 13th April 1868, and had its street level building at the corner of Finchley Road and Queen's Grove.

The station changed little over the years, even after the line was electrified at the beginning of 1905, although its platforms were lengthened in the early 1930s.

It was seemingly little used by this time, as its opening hours had been substantially reduced from 1st October 1929.

The new tube station at St. John's Wood on the Bakerloo Line Extension between Baker Street and Finchley Road was opened on 20th November 1939. Marlborough Road, being rendered superfluous, was closed from the same date.

The street level building as seen from Finchley Road in the early years of the twentieth century.

This is the only view known to the author which shows the platforms at Marlborough Road station whilst they were still in use. It dates from the late 1930s and includes a Metropolitan Railway nameboard on the right. The photographer was standing beneath the glazed overall roof and the slight fuzziness possibly indicates that the camera was hand-held. Nevertheless he seems to have attracted the attention of a member of staff who can be seen walking purposefully towards him.

The platforms were removed some time after closure, but the overall roof, which had also been a feature at St. John's Wood Road and Swiss Cottage, survived in a derelict condition for many years. This photograph was taken in 1966 and looks towards Baker Street.

This view dates from 1966 and shows the Finchley Road elevation of the street level building, with part of the skeletal overall roof remains on the left.

The overall roof disappeared soon after the top photograph was taken, but the street level building survived. It was converted into a restaurant in the early 1970s and although there have been changes of management, it continues to serve this purpose today.

Swiss Cottage

When opened on 13th April 1868, Swiss Cottage was the terminus of the Metropolitan & Saint John's Wood Railway. This ceased to be the case after 30th June 1879, when the line was extended to West Hampstead, although the station remained largely unaltered.

In the 1920s however, the Metropolitan Railway decided to demolish the original street level building on the west side of Finchley Road, and replace it with a shopping arcade incorporating the station entrances. A little later, the platforms, which by then were completely in tunnel, were extended to take eight car trains.

When the Bakerloo Extension between Baker Street and Finchley Road was opened, the LPTB intended to retain the former Metropolitan station at Swiss Cottage as an interchange, but the connection proved to be short lived, as closure came from 18th August 1940, although the street level entrances were retained as access to the Bakerloo Line.

A technically poor, but possibly unique view of the platforms at the Metropolitan Railway's Swiss Cottage station, taken in the late 1930s. The photographer was obviously reliant upon available light and did not use a tripod so the result was marred by 'camera shake', but despite this he has given us a valuable impression of something which otherwise might not have been recorded. Remains of the platforms can still be glimpsed from passing trains.

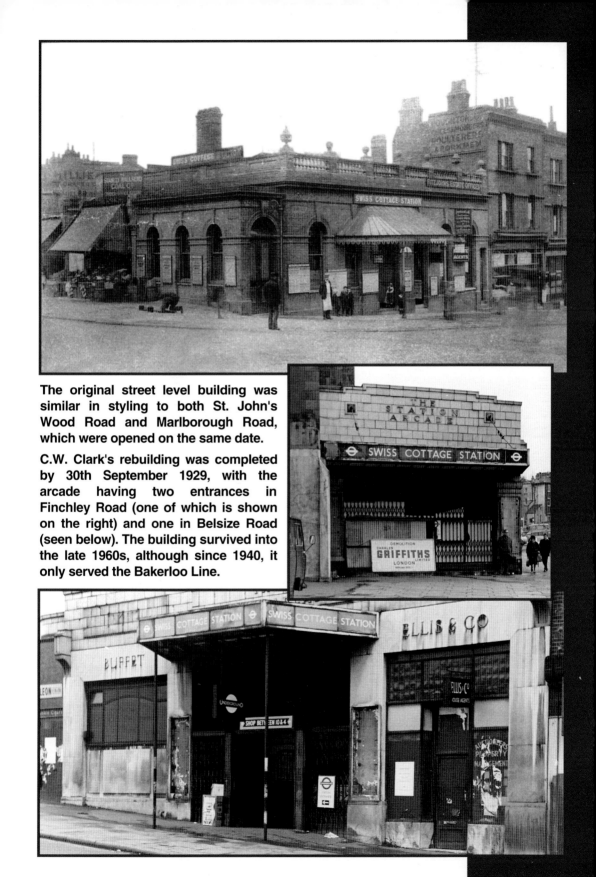

The original street level building was similar in styling to both St. John's Wood Road and Marlborough Road, which were opened on the same date.

C.W. Clark's rebuilding was completed by 30th September 1929, with the arcade having two entrances in Finchley Road (one of which is shown on the right) and one in Belsize Road (seen below). The building survived into the late 1960s, although since 1940, it only served the Bakerloo Line.

Preston Road for Uxendon

On 21st May 1908, the Metropolitan Railway opened a halt on the east side of Preston Road largely to serve the Uxendon Shooting School Club.

It consisted of two 260ft platforms, with small shelters on either side, and a booking office at street level.

At first the surrounding district was still fairly rural, and trains only called when requested. This sometimes resulted in drivers failing to notice waiting passengers, and passing by without stopping. Therefore it was arranged that when passengers wished to join a train, they would be accompanied by the booking clerk, who had to leave his office, then descend to the appropriate platform with a red flag.

As the area developed, it became apparent that the facilities offered by the halt were less than ideal, so improved premises were planned. In 1929, the Metropolitan Railway acquired Parliamentary Authority to widen its formation between Wembley Park and Harrow-on-the-Hill from two tracks to four. Whilst work was underway, a new station, with an island platform was erected at Preston Road to serve the local lines on the opposite side of the bridge. The new up platform was brought into use on 22nd November 1931, followed by the down on 3rd January 1932, and from this date, the original halt was officially closed.

The simple wooden halt at Preston Road for Uxendon, looking towards Harrow-on-the-Hill in its final days, with work in progress on the new local lines and replacement station. After closure on 3rd January 1932, the halt was completely demolished, and no traces now remain.

Beyond Aylesbury

On 23rd September 1868, a small independent company opened a line to link the Great Western Railway at Aylesbury with Verney Junction on the route between Bletchley and Buckingham. It was known as the Aylesbury & Buckingham Railway, and may have remained a purely local affair, had it not have been for the intervention of the Metropolitan Railway chairman, Sir Edward William Watkin. Watkin, whose railway involvement was not restricted to the Metropolitan, had aspirations to transform London's pioneer underground route into a main line. The Met was eventually extended to its own station in Brook Street, Aylesbury on 1st September 1892, but was later connected to the GWR station, therefore allowing Brook Street to be closed. Local Metropolitan services began operating to Verney Junction on 1st April 1894, with through trains between Verney Junction and Baker Street following on 1st January 1897.

From 1st December 1899, the Metropolitan took over the operation of a branch linking Quainton Road with Brill. This originated as the Wotton Tramway, and had served a sparsely populated area since passenger services were introduced in 1872.

Watkin's dream to turn the Metropolitan into a main line railway never succeeded, although in June 1910, a pair of Pullman cars, named *Mayflower* and *Galatea* were introduced on certain 'long distance' services, including some on the Verney Junction line. These vehicles remained in service until October 1939, but by then both the Verney and Brill branches had succumbed to closure. The Quainton Road-Brill service was abandoned from 1st December 1935, and regular passenger trains ceased to link Aylesbury with Verney Junction after 6th July 1936.

The former junction station at Quainton Road was used by British Railways until March 1963, and now accommodates the Buckinghamshire Railway Centre, with its collection of locomotives and rolling stock.

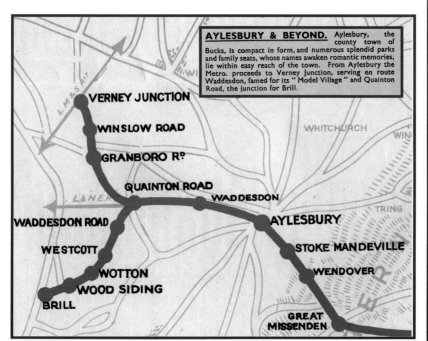

AYLESBURY & BEYOND. Aylesbury, the county town of Bucks, is compact in form, and numerous splendid parks and family seats, whose names awaken romantic memories, lie within easy reach of the town. From Aylesbury the Metro. proceeds to Verney Junction, serving en route Waddesdon, famed for its " Model Village " and Quainton Road, the junction for Brill.

Part of a Metropolitan Railway map showing the Aylesbury area. From 10th September 1961, all London Transport trains terminated at Amersham, leaving the section west of there to British Railways services to and from Marylebone. The former Great Central Railway main line, which is shown as a westward pointing arrow from Quainton Road closed in September 1966.

Quainton Road was served by both Brill and Verney trains, but when these ceased all that remained were the workings to and from Marylebone, latterly operated by British Railways. This view was taken in 1969 and looks towards Aylesbury. The Brill platform was behind the fence on the right.

In its final days the Brill branch proved popular with photographers and other railway enthusiasts who visited the line to sample its unique atmosphere. At this time the services were operated by old Metropolitan locomotives made redundant from central London by electrification in the early years of the twentieth century and one of these, No 41, is seen hauling a single coach branch train at Wood Siding.

The stations on the branch were very basic affairs including the Brill terminus which is seen here. There were ideas to extend the route to Oxford, and although these failed to materialise, ownership of the branch was transferred to the Oxford & Aylesbury Tramway in 1894, before later becoming part of the Met.

The line between Aylesbury and Verney Junction was originally single, but a second track was brought into use from 1st January 1897. The route continued to be used by freight traffic until 1947, although from 1940 all trains used the former up line, as the other track had been converted into a long siding. This is Grandborough Road station during demolition.

Verney Junction took its name from a local landowner, and was located in a very rural area. Two of its platform faces were used by Bletchley - Oxford trains whilst the other accommodated the Met. This view looks east and shows the former Metropolitan side in December 1967, after its track had been lifted. The other face of the island was still in use at the time, but complete closure came soon after when the Bletchley - Oxford service was withdrawn from 1st January 1968.

King's Cross St. Pancras

The original Metropolitan Railway station at King's Cross opened with the first section of the line on 10th January 1863, and had its entrance on the east side of Grays Inn Road. It remained little altered until 1911/12, when LCC tramway electrification work resulted in a replacement street level building being provided at the corner of Pentonville Road and Kings Cross Bridge. At the same time, the fine but ageing overall roof was removed, and umbrella awnings were erected instead.

When opened, the station was named simply King's Cross, but in 1925 it became King's Cross & St. Pancras. A further renaming took place in 1933, when the "&" was dropped, shortening the title to King's Cross St. Pancras.

The LPTB decided to close the Circle Line platforms, and replace them with a new station to the west, which would allow better interchange with the Northern and Piccadilly lines. The platforms used by LMSR and LNER trains on the north side of the premises would not be affected however, and therefore remain open.

The station was damaged by enemy action in October 1940, but the Circle Line platforms did not officially close until 14th March the following year, when their replacements were opened.

The remaining part of the station was completely closed in 1979, but reopened as King's Cross Midland City on 11th July 1983. It was renamed King's Cross Thameslink on 16th May 1988, and continued as such until being replaced by new low level platforms at St. Pancras International on Sunday 9th December 2007.

An eastbound train passes the disused Circle Line platforms at the original Metropolitan Railway King's Cross station on 12th September 1971. At the time, the westbound face of the island seen on the right, was used by British Rail Eastern and London Midland Region services

Above : **The Widened Lines side of King's Cross station is seen here in 1978, with the abandoned Circle Line platforms behind the fence on the left.**

Right : **In connection with the alterations of 1911/12, a separate Widened Lines entrance was opened in Pentonville Road, a little to the east of the main building. This view dates from the 1970s and includes the BR 'King's Cross Local Lines' nameboard which it then carried. The entrance was subsequently rebuilt and enlarged when the station became known as 'King's Cross Midland City'.**

In addition to the enlarged street level building, the early 1980s modifications also brought a rear wall on the down side to separate the premises from the Circle Line tracks along with new platform roofing. This view looks west and was taken in November 2007.

Uxbridge

The original terminus at Uxbridge was opened on 4th July 1904, and until 1st January the following year, when public electric services began, it was served by Metropolitan Railway steam trains.

It was situated off the south-eastern side of Belmont Road, and comprised two platforms. It was laid out in the manner of a through station, in anticipation of the line being extended to High Wycombe, but this never took place, and it remained a terminus to the end of its days.

From 1st March 1910, the Metropolitan services were joined by those of the Metropolitan District Railway, but from 23rd October 1933, the latter were replaced by the Piccadilly Line.

The station was not very well located for the town centre, and was replaced by completely new premises in the High Street on 4th December 1938.

The original terminus was used for a number of years as a warehouse, but its site was subsequently redeveloped.

The main building of the Metropolitan Railway's Uxbridge terminus survived for many years and is seen here in the 1960s.

The station comprised two platforms, with the main building on the down side and a fairly basic shelter on the up. This view looks towards the buffer stops and includes a Metropolitan Railway diamond type nameboard on the right.

Stockwell

Built as the southern terminus of the pioneering City & South London Railway, Stockwell station was brought into public use on 18th December 1890.

Originally the company, then known as the City of London & Southwark Subway, intended its line for cable haulage, and Stockwell was planned as having a single track, with a platform either side. With the subsequent change to electric traction this was changed however, and it opened with two tracks served by a central island.

In July 1890, the company received Parliamentary authority to extend its route to Clapham Common, and Stockwell ceased to be a terminus on 3rd June 1900.

Originally the line was worked with locomotives, but these were later replaced by conventional Underground stock. As part of the modernisation programme, Stockwell closed on 29th November 1923, and did not reopen until 1st December the following year. During this time, new platforms were constructed in twin tunnels, south of the original, and the former island was abandoned. Its site is still visible from a passing train.

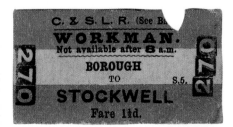

The CSLR was officially opened by HRH The Prince of Wales (later King Edward VII) on 4th November 1890, but public traffic did not commence until the following month. Here the royal party is seen after arrival at Stockwell.

King William Street

Although the City terminus of the world's first electric tube railway was ceremonially opened by HRH The Prince of Wales on 4th November 1890, public traffic did not start until 18th December due to various technical problems.

In keeping with the original intention to use cable haulage, King William Street station was laid out with a single track between two platforms, but this layout soon proved impractical.

In addition, the station's approaches from beneath the Thames involved sharp curves and crippling gradients, so within just two years of opening, the company decided to extend the line northwards to Moorgate Street, and cut out King William Street altogether.

To ease operational difficulties, the station underwent alterations in 1895, when it was provided with two tracks and an island platform, but it closed from 25th February 1900 when the new extension, which left the original alignment just north of Borough, was brought into use.

The station's entrance was incorporated within an existing office building at No 46 King William Street. It is seen soon after closure, with a sign on the right offering the recently vacated premises for letting.

The derelict station at King William Street is seen here around 1930. The platform had been partially removed, but the signal box and the remains of some gas lighting survived, together with evidence of the station's name, which was still visible on the tiling.

TheUnderground Group decided to dispose of No 46 King William Street for redevelopment in 1930, so a number of journalists were invited along to provide publicity. Various photographs were taken, including this one which shows a workman shining his light towards a surviving semaphore signal.

The building was demolished in 1933 and redeveloped as an office block known as Regis House. In 1940, its owners took out a tenancy on the former station tunnel and converted it into a two-level air raid shelter, of which the upper section is seen above, with its original 1890 ceramic tiling still in place.

A section of stairway remained largely unaltered and still displayed the style of waistband tiling featured by the CSLR on its earliest stations.

To the left are the stairs linking the upper and lower shelters, complete with wartime *'Careless Talk Costs Lives'* posters by the satirical artist Cyril Kenneth Bird, better known as *'Fougasse'*.

The present Regis House carries a plaque to commemorate the historic station which once occupied the site.

City Road

City Road station opened with the City & South London Railway extension from Moorgate Street to Angel on 17th November 1901.

It was located between Old Street and Angel, and consisted of two platforms. Its surface building stood at the corner of City Road and Moreland Street, and passengers gained access to the trains by means of two lifts.

It was never well used, and as early as 1908, the company were considering its closure. It remained open however, but its days were numbered.

The CSLR became part of the Underground Group on 1st January 1913, and so that standardised rolling stock could be used, the bore of the running tunnels had to be enlarged. The section of line north of Moorgate Street closed for rebuilding on 9th August 1922, and although this subsequently reopened, City Road remained closed. The platforms were later removed, and the former platform tunnels were converted for use as an air raid shelter in 1941.

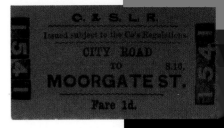

The tower of a ventilation shaft was added to the street level building after closure, but otherwise it remained little altered for many years. Partial demolition took place around the 1970s, but a fragment of it still survives.

Above : **This is the passageway which once led from the lower lift landing to the platforms at City Road.**

Right : **A relic of the period when the station was used as an air raid shelter.**

Below : **Although the platforms have long-since disappeared at City Road, their site is still visible from passing trains.**

NOTICE

PILLOWS, RUGS OR BLANKETS MUST NOT BE LEFT IN THIS SHELTER. ANY PERSONAL BELONGINGS OF THIS KIND FOUND IN THE SHELTER WILL BE IMMEDIATELY REMOVED.

By Order.

South Kentish Town

Prior to opening on 22nd June 1907, this station on the Charing Cross Euston & Hampstead Railway was known as Castle Road. In fact, this was the name which was fired onto the platform tiling, but the company changed its mind, and painted it out before services commenced.

It was never well used, and when it closed during a strike at Lots Road power station on 5th June 1924, it never reopened.

In 1940, the former platform tunnels were adapted for use as air raid shelters, and equipped with bunks and a first aid post. These fittings were removed when hostilities ended however, and the station returned to its slumber.

The platforms were removed at an unknown date, but according to an article in *The Railway World* for December 1954, the wall tiling could *"still be seen from passing trains."*

The street level building, designed by Leslie W. Green still stands, and is currently used as commercial premises. It is located at the corner of Kentish Town Road and Castle Place, and externally has changed little since closure. This view shows it while completely disused in the 1970s.

South Kentish Town was a typical Leslie W. Green station and shared many common features. These photographs show the stairway which led from the booking hall. As can be seen, the walls were clad to waist height in green tiling, topped by a decorative frieze in the style now referred to generally as art-nouveau.

Down below, the lower sections of the passageway walls were clad in cream and brown tiling, which was also featured throughout much of the station, including the platform tunnels.

The lifts were removed many years ago and the shafts were plugged, but the lower lift landing retained many of its original features.

Soon after closure, an absent minded passenger alighted at the station as his train stopped at a signal. The platform was presumably unlit, so how he made the mistake is anyone's guess. However, before he realised, the train set off and left him in the dark. He was soon picked up, but the incident resulted in some humorous verses in the TOT staff magazine, written and illustrated by F.H. Stingemore. This presumably came to the attention of John (later Sir John) Betjeman, who used it as inspiration for a late night radio broadcast in 1951.

At track level the station tunnels can be seen from a passing train between Camden Town and Kentish Town, but their tiled walls have largely been obliterated by paint. This view shows one of the original 'Castle Road' name panels, when it was briefly exposed some years ago. As can be seen, the platforms have been removed.

North End

Passengers travelling between Hampstead and Golders Green on today's Northern Line may look out into the tunnel, and see what appears to be the remains of a disused station. In fact, what they are seeing is the site of a station which was partially constructed by the Charing Cross Euston & Hampstead Railway, but abandoned before completion. It was to be named North End, and would have had a street level building on the north side of Hampstead Way, opposite Wyldes Farmhouse.

The fact that much of its immediate surroundings consisted of conserved open land meant that there was little chance of development in the area, so the project was cancelled. By this time, some work had been carried out at track level, but nothing was erected above.

The unfinished station later became known by staff as 'Bull & Bush' after the nearby public house featured in Florrie Forde's famous music hall song.

A floodgate control room was installed there in the 1950s, when access from the street was finally provided, although the site originally intended for its building was sold for residential use in 1927.

Although no work was carried out above ground, the station tunnels were constructed, complete with cross-passages and partly finished stairways. It also seems that the platforms were erected as a writer in the *Railway Observer* for July 1954 recalled that their *"edges were cut back"* about 1933 *"with the presumed object of reducing maintenance"*. This view shows the lower section of an unfinished stairway.

An illustration of *'The Firs, North End, Hampstead'* appeared on the front of this early leaflet.

York Road

Opened on 15th December 1906, York Road was one of the original stations on the Great Northern Piccadilly & Brompton Railway.

It was located between King's Cross and Caledonian Road, and had its entrance at the corner of York Road (now York Way) and Bingfield Street.

Even in its early days it appears to have been little used, and some trains began to pass without stopping from October 1909. Sunday services were withdrawn after 5th May 1918, but apart from an extended period of disuse brought about by the General Strike in 1926, the station remained open for weekday traffic until 19th September 1932, when it was permanently closed.

The street level building, designed by Leslie W. Green, still survives and is a fine example of the architect's work. Its frontage was renovated in 1989, and since then the remains of the original lettering, including the station name, have been clearly visible. This view dates from 1966 when the premises were being used by a printing company.

The platform tunnels were decorated in cream tiling detailed in maroon and dark orange, with white backing to the name panels. This extremely rare view shows the station whilst still in use, possibly around the time of closure.

A view of the northbound platform taken in 1995, showing the signal cabin which remained in use until 25th April 1964.

A few small areas of original tiling can just about be glimpsed from passing trains, including this section which is near the old signal cabin.

Although a few sections remain untouched, the majority of platform tiling has been obscured by matt grey paint for many years, including the name panels although one of these was briefly exposed in 1995 along with an adjoining 'No Exit' cartouche, as seen in this photograph.

Aldwych

The station was opened as Strand by the Great Northern Piccadilly & Brompton Railway on 30th November 1907, but was renamed Aldwych on 9th May 1915.

It was the terminus of a 573 yard branch line from Holborn, and although well patronised by theatre goers in its early days, its fortunes soon fell into decline.

One of its two platforms was little used after 1912, and was later closed completely.

Services over the branch were suspended during the Second World War from 22nd September 1940 until 1st July 1946. During these years the tunnels were used as an air raid shelter, and also to store art treasures from the British Museum.

The need for lift replacement hastened the station's demise, and final closure came after traffic on Friday 30th September 1994.

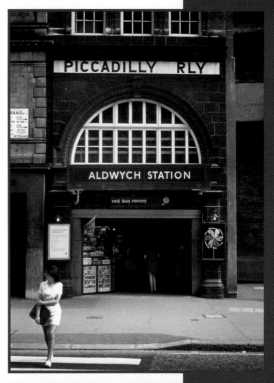

The station occupied an L shaped site which previously accommodated the Royal Strand Theatre and, as can be seen from these 1970s photographs, had entrances onto both the Strand itself (top) and Surrey Street (bottom). The original appearance of the latter was altered some time after the mid-1920s, when replacement windows were installed at first floor level. A tiled panel showing the original station name survived behind the canopy of the Strand entrance and was restored after closure.

In common with the majority of stations on the Yerkes' group of lines, the platform tiling included fired-on name panels. These were covered-up to avoid confusion after renaming, but sometimes, when the walls were stripped of posters, the original title was exposed and remained visible for a while.

```
5        8792
LONDON  PASSENGER
TRANSPORT  BOARD
      ALDWYCH
3rd Cl   to   (Auto,1)
 2ᵈ      Kings Cross &
              St. Pancras
         Hyde Park Cnr.
         Regents Park
         Warren Street
         Waterloo (Ch'ge
         Holb'rn(Kingsw'y)
         & Leicester Sq.)
         Euston    Bank
         Marble Arch
         Angel
         or intermediately
 2ᵈ
ALDWYCH
5        8792
```

As the station neared completion, the company decided that it would only be served by short trains, so the Holborn end of its platforms remained untiled, as seen in this view from the 1990s.

Being relatively little used throughout much of its existence, Aldwych was often hired by film makers and it has appeared under various guises in both features and programmes made for television. This view, taken after closure, includes some reproduction vintage posters on the left which were presumably added for filming purposes.

Down Street

Because of problems at its planning stage, work on constructing Down Street station was late in starting, and therefore its opening was delayed. It was brought into use on 15th March 1907, three months after public services on the Great Northern Piccadily & Brompton Railway had commenced, but from the outset traffic was very light.

It was close to both Dover Street (now Green Park), and Hyde Park Corner, which were the stations on either side, and it served a district where, even in its early days, people had access to private transport.

Certain trains began to pass without stopping after 1909, and Sunday services were withdrawn from 5th May 1918. Complete closure came fourteen years later, on 22nd May 1932.

Leslie W. Green's street level building still survives and has changed little since this view was taken in 1966.

Passenger access from street level was by means of two Otis electric lifts, which were located within a single 60.68ft deep shaft. These were removed after closure, although a small lift was later fitted for wartime use. This view looks from the base of the liftshaft towards the passages which led to the platforms.

The tiling in and around the passageways leading from the lower lift landing continues to show its original colour scheme and part of a fired-on 'To The Trains' sign, complete with directional arrow remains visible.

Immediately prior to the Second World War, the premises were adapted as bomb-proof office accommodation and became the headquarters of the Railway Executive Committee. Down Street was also used by the War Cabinet on occasion and Winston Churchill was reputedly sometimes seen walking across Green Park, en-route from Whitehall. When hostilities ended, the office partitions which had been erected within the passageways were removed, but traces of them remain on the floor as seen here.

Original tiling also remains visible on the two stairways, one of which was intended as an entrance and the other as an exit. The station colour scheme was maroon and cream and the tiling pattern at platform level was quite elaborate, although much of this was obscured by grey paint when the premises were adapted for their wartime use.

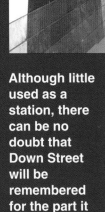

The former platform areas are largely hidden from passing trains by brick walls, but a few sections of original tiling escaped being painted over, including this fragment adjoining a headwall on the westbound side, complete with a 'No Exit' cartouche.

Although little used as a station, there can be no doubt that Down Street will be remembered for the part it played in the Second World War.

Sadly little appears to remain of the name panels, although part of one, largely obscured by paint, survives behind a wartime door on the eastbound side.

Brompton Road

Brompton Road was situated between Knightsbridge and South Kensington, on the Great Northern, Piccadilly & Brompton Railway, and opened with the line on 15th December 1906.

Although convenient for the Brompton Oratory and the Victoria & Albert Museum, it was never well patronised, and from October 1909 some trains passed without stopping. Before leaving either Knightsbridge or South Kensington, staff on these services would yell *"Passing Brompton Road!"*, and this call became so familiar that it gave its name to a West End farce in 1928.

The station closed from 4th May 1926 due to the General Strike, and did not reopen until 4th October the same year. When first brought back into use, trains only called on weekdays, but Sunday services were restored on 2nd January 1927.

By then however, its days were numbered, and when the newly rebuilt Knightsbridge station was provided with an additional entrance fairly nearby, Brompton Road closed from 30th July 1934.

Just prior to the outbreak of the Second World War, the street level building, together with liftshafts and certain passageways was sold to the War Office for use by the 1st Anti-Aircraft Division.

The street level building occupied an L-shaped site. The frontage (above) included both entrance and exit and faced onto Brompton Road itself. This was demolished to facilitate road widening in 1972, but the side elevation in Cottage Place, which does not seem to have been intended as a means of public access (right), continues to stand.

The platform areas at Brompton Road remained LPTB property, although they were leased to the government during the Second World War and used as office and dormitory accommodation. They were largely walled off from passing trains, but retained their tiling and much of this still survives.

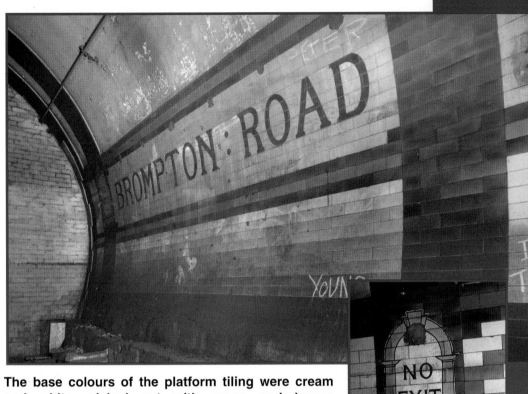

The base colours of the platform tiling were cream and white, picked out with green and brown patterning. The surviving sections include examples of name panels, along with various other fired-on signs as seen here. The view at bottom right shows a section of the emergency stairs.

Northfields & Little Ealing

On 16th April 1908, the Metropolitan District Railway opened Northfield (Ealing) Halt between South Ealing and Boston Road (now Boston Manor) on the Hounslow line.

As suburban housing along this route had been slow to develop, the premises were very basic, and comprised a street level ticket hut, serving a pair of 300ft platforms.

With traffic increasing however, the halt proved inadequate, so it was rebuilt as a full station, and renamed Northfields & Little Ealing on 11th December 1911.

In time, it was decided to extend Piccadilly Line trains to Hounslow West, but before this could be done, a number of improvements had to be made. Amongst these was the laying of additional tracks between Acton Town and Northfields, and the provision of a new depot near Boston Manor. To facilitate these changes, it proved necessary to resite Northfields station eastwards to the opposite side of the road.

The new station was opened, albeit still unfinished, on 19th May 1932. Its predecessor closed on the same date, and was subsequently demolished.

Northfields & Little Ealing station after its 1911 rebuilding, looking towards Acton Town as a Hounslow train approaches the westbound platform.

Osterley

Osterley station was opened by the Hounslow & Metropolitan Railway on 1st May 1883, but its services were provided by the Metropolitan District Railway from the outset.

Its street level building was located on the west side of Thornbury Road, and from here, stairs descended to the platforms below.

It is known that the board on the frontage displayed the name as 'Osterley Park and Spring Grove', but it appears that this was never shown on MDR tickets, even if variations of it sometimes appeared on through bookings from other companies.

The original Osterley station closed on 25th March 1934, when it was replaced by new premises facing onto the Great West Road.

The original Osterley station is seen in this view, which dates from 1930 and looks east. The platforms still exist, but the awnings and associated structures are understood to have been demolished in 1957.

The street level building continues to stand and has changed little since closure. This photograph was taken in 1966.

Hounslow Town

The Hounslow & Metropolitan Railway opened this terminus on 1st May 1883. It was originally called Hounslow, but was renamed Hounslow Town the following year. The company wanted to extend the line to form a link with the London & South Western Railway, but the LSWR objected and the scheme failed to materialise.

When the HMR was extended to Hounslow Barracks (later Hounslow West), its original terminus was deemed superfluous, so it closed from 1st April 1886. A subsequent change of heart resulted in it being reopened on 1st March 1903 and the branch was included in the Metropolitan District Railway's electrification scheme.

An additional spur was added to provide access from the Hounslow Barracks end, and this was opened to coincide with the new electric service on 13th June 1905. The method of running all trains by way of the old terminus proved unsatisfactory however, so they were diverted onto the direct line and the branch was closed permanently from 2nd May 1909.

Hounslow Town was later demolished, and redeveloped as a 'bus garage, but the site of the original junction is still discernible on the south side of today's Piccadilly Line between Osterley and Hounslow East.

This section of a Metropolitan District Railway map of August 1907 shows the route taken by MDR trains in the years immediately following electrification.

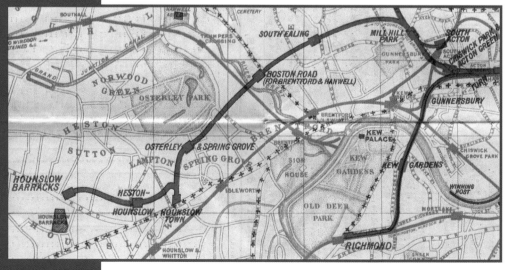

The direct route between Osterley and Heston Hounslow, was out of regular public use from 13th June 1905 until 2nd May 1909, and was therefore not included on this map.

During its first period of closure, Hounslow Town station became semi-derelict and by 1901 it was reported that *"the flooring of the two platforms is gone (except under the covered portion) and the beams are fast decaying."* The premises were tidied up for their 1903 reopening, but as they were only to be served by short trains there was no need to rebuild the platforms to their original length. This photograph is believed to show the station shortly before it closed permanently, with a train departing for Mill Hill Park, which was renamed Acton Town in 1910.

This photograph shows the exterior immediately after closure, with posters directing passengers to the replacemement station, which was located on the direct line. Although the replacement opened as Hounslow Town, it was renamed Hounslow East in 1925.

Hounslow West

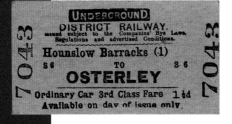

This view shows Hounslow West terminus as it appeared around the 1950s. The original platform can be seen to the left, but the island in the foreground was added in 1926.

Originally named Hounslow Barracks, the station was opened on 21st July 1884 as terminus of the Hounslow & Metropolitan Railway.

It lay at the end of an extension which diverged from the original Hounslow Town line at Lampton Junction, and consisted of a single platform. In fact, the line which served it was single, although the formation was built to a sufficient width for it to be doubled at a later stage if required. This subsequently took place, but the final stretch into Hounslow Barracks remained single until 1926.

The route was electrified by the Metropolitan District Railway in 1905, but it would be some years before any major improvements were made at the station. The first sign of change came on 1st December 1925 when it was renamed Hounslow West, then during the following year it was substantially enlarged.

Piccadilly Line services were extended to serve Hounslow West on 13th March 1933, and for over three decades shared the station with the District Line. District trains were withdrawn from the route after 9th October 1964 however, and thereafter it was served by the Piccadilly Line only.

An extension of the branch to serve Heathrow Airport necessitated the provision of a through station on the new route. The old terminal platforms were last used on 11th July 1975, and were subsequently demolished to provide space for a car park, although the main building, completed in 1931 to the design of Charles Holden, remains in use.

Park Royal & Twyford Abbey

The original Park Royal station was located on the south side of Twyford Abbey Road, and opened on 23rd June 1903. The premises were very basic, and comprised a pair of wooden platforms linked by a footbridge.

The station was intended to serve the 102 acre Royal Agricultural Showground which lay immediately to its east.

The route between Hanger Lane Junction and South Harrow on which the station was situated, was served by the Metropolitan District Railway, but from 4th July 1932 it became part of the Piccadilly Line. In preparation for this change, it was decided to build a new Park Royal station about 30 chains to the east, and then close the original. The new premises were a vast improvement on those in Twyford Abbey Road, and were brought into use on 6th July 1931 as a direct replacement for them.

Being a fairly flimsy structure, the original station was easily demolished, and no tangible traces of it now remain.

Although the original station was officially named Park Royal & Twyford Abbey, the full title did not appear on its final nameboards, nor seemingly on MDR tickets which were issued there.
This view shows the eastbound platform, with the building accommodating the ticket office to the left.

Uxbridge Road

Uxbridge Road was opened by the West London Railway on 1st November 1869, and was located north of Kensington Addison Road (now Olympia) near the site of an earlier WLR Shepherds Bush station which had opened and closed in 1844.

In addition to West London Line trains between Clapham Junction and Willesden Junction, Uxbridge Road was also served by the Metropolitan Railway, which reached it by means of a connecting spur off the Hammersmith & City route to the south-west of Latimer Road. This spur opened on 1st July 1864, and for many years formed part of 'The Middle Circle'. By way of this, Metropolitan trains could diverge near Latimer Road, then after calling at Uxbridge Road arrive at Addison Road.

Uxbridge Road station was closed from 21st October 1940, with the spur losing its passenger services the previous day. The spur was retained for freight traffic until 1st March 1954, but was subsequently lifted.

The Latimer Road - Addison Road route, together with Uxbridge Road, last appeared on an Underground pocket map in 1947, seven years after the station closed.

In September 2008 a new station, named Shepherds Bush, was opened on part of the old Uxbridge Road site for use of London Overground services between Willesden Junction and Clapham Junction.

The platforms and attendant structures had been completely demolished by the mid-1960s, leaving just the erstwhile street level building and a pair of truncated stairways.

The street level building, to the east of Shepherds Bush Green, lingered on for a few more years, until it was demolished in connection with road alterations which took place in the early 1970s. Both these views date from 1967.

Hammersmith Grove Road

Opened as Hammersmith by the London & South Western Railway on 1st January 1869, this station was located on the line linking Kensington Addison Road (now Olympia) with Richmond.

Services were initially only provided by the LSWR, but from 1st June 1870, a connection off the Hammersmith & City Line allowed the operation of GWR trains from Bishop's Road Paddington to Richmond. These called at the LSWR Hammersmith station, but were withdrawn after just a few months on 1st November 1870. From 1st October 1877 however, the link began to be used by Metropolitan Railway Moorgate Street - Richmond trains, with GWR services making their reappearance in 1894. Passengers were subsequently wooed away by the new electric tramways, and the connection between the H&C and LSWR was finally closed from 1st January 1911.

Hammersmith station, by now in possession of the suffix 'Grove Road', or as it was sometimes known 'The Grove', continued to be used by LSWR services until closure on 5th June 1916.

Since 1877, the Metropolitan District Railway had operated over the LSWR route beyond Hammersmith to reach Richmond, and these services continued. Therefore only the section of line between Kensington and Hammersmith was actually closed, and although there was talk of bringing it back into use, it was subsequently lifted.

Passengers on today's District and Piccadilly Line trains can still see parts of the disused viaduct to the north of the formation between Hammersmith and Ravenscourt Park stations. The link with the H&C has long since disappeared however, as has the station at Hammersmith Grove Road.

Apart from the main building, which was brick, Hammersmith Grove Road was largely constructed of wood as seen from this view which looks towards Kensington shortly after closure. The station was linked to the north end of Hammersmith terminus on the H&C by means of a footbridge, which led from the building on the right.

District Outposts

On 1st March 1883, the Metropolitan District Railway commenced working between Mansion House and Windsor, by way of a connection onto the GWR at Ealing. The service initially comprised eleven weekday trains each way, with nine on Sundays, but there was little demand, so it was cut back to four in either direction on 1st October 1884. It was withdrawn completely from 30th September 1885, and track alterations at Ealing Broadway in 1898/9 eliminated the connection completely. This view shows MDR 4-4-0T No 42 carrying a Windsor destination board. Unfortunately, the background has been painted out, but the photograph is thought to have been taken at Mill Hill Park (now Acton Town).

MDR locomotives L5 and L3 arriving at Barking with the 10.27am Ealing Broadway to Southend through train on 12th October 1930. The train is formed of ex-LTSR corridor stock which was built specially for the service in 1911.

From 1st June 1910 until 1st October 1939, a service of through trains operated between Ealing Broadway and Southend. These travelled by way of the Whitechapel & Bow Railway, which had opened in 1902, and were hauled by a pair of MDR electric locomotives, generally as far as Barking where an engine from the London, Tilbury & Southend Railway would take over.

Northern City Line

Until 5th October 1975 the Northern City Line was part of the London Underground network.

It had opened as the Great Northern & City Railway on 14th February 1904 and stretched for a distance of 3.42 miles from Finsbury Park to Moorgate. As it was intended to provide a physical connection with the Great Northern Railway at Finsbury Park, the line was built with 16ft diameter tunnels instead of 12ft which had been adopted as standard on other tube routes. This would have permitted the through running of suburban trains, but the connection failed to materialise and it would be many decades before the idea became reality. The GNCR was in tunnel for most of its length and had intermediate stations at Drayton Park, Highbury, Essex Road and Old Street, although Highbury was not brought into use until 28th June 1904.

The Northern City Line as featured on a Metropolitan Railway pocket map of the 1920s.

Despite early hopes, the GNCR was not a great financial success and, following an Act of Parliament, it was taken over by the Metropolitan Railway, which began operating services on 1st July 1913. The route became part of the LPTB in 1933 and in the following year was renamed the Northern City Line.

Under the 1935-40 New Works plan it was intended to revive the idea of a connection with the high level tracks at Finsbury Park and extend Underground services over certain ex-GNR branches. The work was interrupted by the Second World War however and plans involving the Northern City Line were abandoned.

In connection with Victoria Line construction, Northern City services between Drayton Park and Finsbury Park were withdrawn from 4th October 1964 but they continued working between Drayton Park and Moorgate for a further eleven years until the route was handed over to British Rail for conversion.

At long last, the connection at Finsbury Park became a reality and in 1976, seventy-two years after the route opened, main line rolling stock made its public debut on the Northern City Line.

From 1939 until 1966, the Northern City Line was worked by trains of 'Standard' tube stock, as seen here at Drayton Park in 1966.

East London Line

In the small hours of Sunday 23rd December 2007, the East London Line, linking Whitechapel with New Cross and New Cross Gate, was deleted from the Underground network when it closed for conversion into part of the Overground system.

The route has a fascinating history, which is too complex to cover in detail here, but suffice to say that the first section opened between the original terminus at New Cross *(see page 37)* and what is now Wapping on 7th December 1869. To pass beneath the river the route utilised the existing Thames Tunnel, which had been constructed under the direction of Sir Marc Brunel, assisted by his famous son Isambard, and completed in 1843. The tunnel had originally been used by pedestrians, but was later sold for railway use and officially handed over in 1865.

The line was subsequently provided with additional connections in the New Cross area, but its most notable extension came on 10th April 1876, when services were extended northwards from Wapping to the Great Eastern Railway terminus at Liverpool Street, by way of Shoreditch *(see page 33)*.

From 1882 the line was managed by a Joint Committee formed of five other railways, namely the London Brighton & South Coast, the London Chatham & Dover, the Metropolitan, the Metropolitan District and the South Eastern, with the GER joining three years later.

The line was electrified in 1913, although the scheme did not include a connection with Old Kent Road on the LBSCR, which had been officially closed two years earlier. At the opposite end, the conductor rails stretched no further than Shoreditch, so this became the route's northern terminus.

Whitechapel Low Level opened with the northern extension from Wapping in 1876 and was originally protected from the elements by a glazed overall roof. This view dates from 1968 and shows a train of Q Stock standing at the platform.

The new electric services were operated by the Metropolitan Railway, with some shuttling back and forth between Shoreditch and the two stations at New Cross and others originating from elsewhere on the Metropolitan system, travelling via the St Mary's Curve. Passenger workings over this connection were drastically reduced in the second half of the 1930s and withdrawn completely from 6th October 1941, leaving the line with just the local services which it retained until the end of London Underground ownership.

The East London Line once served as a useful freight link, but with traffic increasingly being transferred to road haulage, the goods trains were no longer needed and they were withdrawn in the 1960s. The connections with the main line network at both ends were subsequently severed, so the only link with the outside world was the St Mary's Curve, which was largely used for empty stock movements.

As part of the Overground system, the East London Line will carry trains from Crystal Palace and West Croydon in the south to Dalston Junction and Highbury in the north-east, therefore transforming it back into the useful cross-town link it was intended to be back in the 1860s.

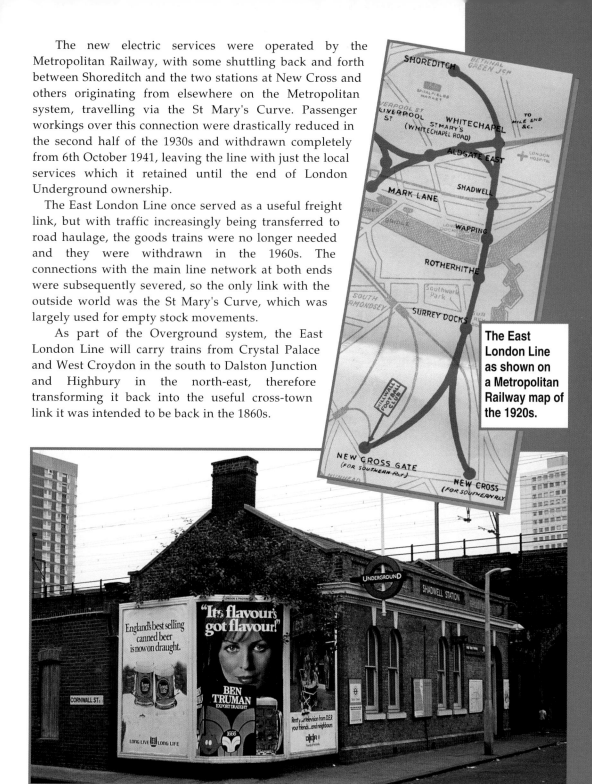

The East London Line as shown on a Metropolitan Railway map of the 1920s.

Shadwell was another station which opened with the northern extension in April 1876. This view shows the street level building in Watney Street, which was replaced by a new entrance in Cable Street in January 1983. The photograph was taken in the early 1970s and includes the British Rail Fenchurch Street line on viaduct behind.

A train of Q Stock is seen entering Surrey Docks in 1970 as it heads towards New Cross Gate. The station opened with the initial section of line in December 1869 and was originally named Deptford Road. The title was expanded to 'Deptford Road for Southwark Park' around March 1890, then altered to Surrey Docks on 17th July 1911. In later years the premises underwent various modifications, including a new street level building in 1981-2 and it received its present name, Surrey Quays, on 24th October 1989.

The last southbound London Underground train to New Cross, the 00.59 ex-Whitechapel, departs from Wapping on 23rd December 2007. The station had opened as 'Wapping & Shadwell' in 1869 and served as a temporary terminus until the northern extension opened seven years later. When the present station at Shadwell opened on 10th April 1876 the suffix became superfluous and was therefore dropped.

The District
Deep Level Line

To relieve pressure on its most overcrowded section, the Metropolitan District Railway contemplated building a deep level tube line between Earl's Court and Mansion House. The scheme was announced in October 1896, and was envisaged to diverge from the existing tracks east of Earl's Court before descending on a 1 in 42 gradient towards Gloucester Road. It would then continue below the sub-surface MDR in a pair of 12ft 6in tubes and eventually terminate at Mansion House. It was to be electrified from the outset, and to speed up services there would be only one intermediate station. This was planned for Charing Cross (now Embankment), where the new platforms would lie 63ft below the original District Line, and these would be connected to the booking hall above by means of hydraulic lifts.

Parliamentary authority was received on 6th August 1897, but the line never materialised in its intended form. At that time, the MDR was still worked by steam, and a change of locomotives would be necessary before trains could continue onto the tube section. Because this would almost certainly cause delays if carried out at Earl's Court, it was suggested that it should take place in a stretch of covered way beneath Cromwell Road. In the event however, the plan was abandoned, although the stretch from South Kensington to Earl's Court was ultimately built as part of the Great Northern Piccadilly & Brompton Railway.

The remaining sections failed to materialise, apart from a 120ft length of station tunnel which was constructed at South Kensington in 1903. This was level with the present westbound Piccadilly Line platform, but before completion it was realised that electrification of the existing MDR would increase the line capacity through the City, and the deep level route would therefore not be required. No further work was carried out, and Parliamentary powers to build between South Kensington and Mansion House were relinquished in 1908.

The unfinished station tunnel at South Kensington, which was tiled in the style used on the various Yerkes' tube lines, served as a signalling school from 1927 to 1939. During the Second World War, part of it was fitted with electronic equipment to record any delayed action bombs which were dropped in the Thames, and threatened to breach underwater tube tunnels.

The Northern Heights

Probably the best known abandoned Underground project is the scheme to extend Northern Line services to Alexandra Palace and Bushey Heath. Both of these had their origins in New Works Plans of the 1930s, and had it not been for the intervention of the Second World War, they would have no doubt materialised.

The plan envisaged the London Passenger Transport Board taking over the former GNR branches to Edgware, High Barnet and Alexandra Palace, and replacing the existing steam workings with tube trains. At Edgware a connection to the existing LPTB station would be laid, and a completely new extension built to serve Brockley Hill, Elstree (later referred to as Elstree South) and Bushey Heath.

Work continued into the early years of the War, but as the Luftwaffe raids on London intensified, the scheme was halted. Tube trains reached High Barnet on 14th April 1940, before the onset of the Blitz, and a year later, on 18th May 1941, they got to Mill Hill East. From then on however the scheme faltered, and the remaining Northern Heights projects were left unfinished.

Post-War Green Belt legislation ruled out developing the area north of Edgware, so the Bushey Heath plan was ultimately scrapped, and the line serving Alexandra Palace was latterly so little used that electrification was not deemed worthwhile. Instead it remained steam worked to the end, and closed from 5th July 1954.

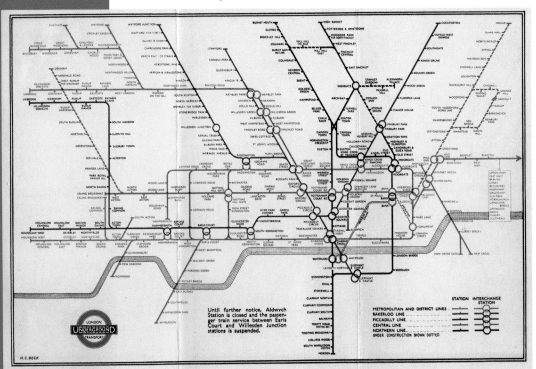

This 1941 edition of the pocket Underground map shows both the Mill Hill East - Bushey Heath extension and the Alexandra Palace branch. These were removed from later issues, but reappeared after the war, before being permanently deleted in 1950 and 1951 respectively. Also included is the Central Line extension to Denham, which was destined to stretch no further than West Ruislip.

Despite electrification, Mill Hill East retained many of its pre-grouping features. Here a train of LPTB 1938 Stock stands at the station in 1966, with the site of a second track to the right. This was laid as part of the pre-war scheme, but lifted after freight services to Edgware ceased in 1964.

Mill Hill The Hale started life as The Hale Halt in 1906, and last saw passenger trains when the branch was closed for electrification on 11th September 1939. It was due for complete rebuilding, but work was aborted in its early stages. The photograph above dates from the 1930s and looks towards Finchley, whilst that to the right was taken in 1966 with a rebuilt section of platform visible beneath the Bunns Lane bridge. The Midland main line from St Pancras crossed above the branch nearby and can be seen in the distance in the 1930s view.

Although a great deal of preparatory work was carried out on the route between Edgware and Bushey Heath, the most notable civil engineering feature was this unfinished viaduct at Brockley Hill. This would have supported the station, and a service road leading into the car park was intended to pass between the two sets of arches. The view dates from the 1950s, and shows the structure before partial demolition. Today only the lower sections survive, and can be seen to the north of Edgware Way.

The line would have passed under Elstree Hill in twin tunnels, as seen here. These served as a rifle range for a while, but were bricked up in August 1953, and have since disappeared. The only other major structure erected for the line was the depot at Aldenham, between Elstree South and Bushey Heath. This was used for aircraft construction during the war, and later became well known for overhauling London's 'buses. It has since been closed and demolished.

The first station out of Finsbury Park heading towards Alexandra Palace was Stroud Green, which opened on 11th April 1881, and had its entrance on the west side of Stapleton Hall Road, just south of the junction with Ferme Park Road. The views above and to the right date from January 1966, and were taken just three months before demolition.

Further on, the line reached Crouch End, which was entered by way of a street level building on the east side of Crouch End Hill, south of the junction with Haslemere Road. The station was opened on 22nd August 1867, and remained largely unaltered, although work was latterly carried out to lower the platform height to enable use by tube services. The trackbed of the line between Finsbury Park and Highgate is now a public footpath, and although the majority of Crouch End station has disappeared, its platforms still remain. The photograph was taken in January 1966.

Highgate station, which had opened with the line from Finsbury Park to Edgware on 22nd August 1867, was substantially modernised in 1940-41 when it received a new Holden designed building on its island platform, reached by a stairway from the Underground booking hall below. The tracks were used for transferring Underground stock between Drayton Park on the Northern City Line and Highgate Wood sidings until 1970. As they were not electrified, the trains had to be hauled by battery locomotives. The track was lifted in 1972, but Highgate station still survived in 2008, albeit derelict and overgrown.

Beyond Highgate, the branch to Alexandra Palace diverged from the High Barnet and Edgware routes, and soon reached Cranley Gardens. This station opened on 2nd August 1902, and is seen here in 1966. Its street level building stood on the west side of Muswell Hill Road, almost opposite the junction with Cranley Gardens itself, but this was demolished along with the platform remains in the late 1960s, when the site was required for redevelopment.

Muswell Hill station was opened on 24th May 1873 and had its entrance on the north side of Muswell Hill itself.This view shows a Finsbury Park to Alexandra Palace train arriving behind an N2 class 0-6-2T shortly before closure. The buildings are thought to have been demolished around 1960, but the overgrown platforms survived a little longer.

The branch terminus comprised a single island platform for much of its existence, and was totally dwarfed by the huge bulk of Alexandra Palace itself which stood alongside. After closure, the platform was demolished, but the street level building, facing onto The Avenue, still survives. The photograph was taken in 1966.

Express Tube Lines

Following the start of the London Blitz in September 1940, the government decided to build a series of deep level air raid shelters, connected to existing tube stations. These would be constructed by the LPTB on behalf of the Ministry of Home Security, on the understanding that when hostilities ceased they could be linked by new tunnels and used to form express tube lines, which had been proposed in the late 1930s.

A number of sites were considered, but eventually the choice fell on St. Paul's, Chancery Lane, Belsize Park, Camden Town, Goodge Street, Oval, Stockwell, Clapham North, Clapham Common and Clapham South. In all instances the shelters would be positioned either parallel to or below existing station tunnels, and comprise a pair of tubes, each with an internal diameter of 16ft 6ins. These would have a length of 1,400ft, and be lined partly with precast concrete and partly with cast iron. Two floors were to be provided in each tunnel, and these would have enough bunks to accommodate 8,000 people, although the initial number was proposed as 9,600.

The scheme was bugged with labour shortages, and the shelter at Oval was abandoned in 1941, after just 250ft of tunnel, plus a few passageways had been built. A little earlier, the authorities responsible for St. Paul's Cathedral objected to tunnelling being undertaken in their immediate vicinity, so work at St. Paul's was halted, and not resumed.

There was progress elsewhere however, and towards the end of 1942, part of the shelter at Goodge Street was fitted out as headquarters for General Eisenhower. The others were also adapted to serve government needs, and it was not until the onset of Hitler's 'V' weapons, that any were opened for public use. The first was at Stockwell on 9th July 1944, and this was followed by Clapham North (13.7.44.), Camden Town (16.7.44.), Clapham South (19.7.44.) and Belsize Park (23.7.44.). The remainder continued to serve government purposes.

After the war, the shelters were adapted to provide overnight accommodation for soldiers on leave, and other large transient groups, as well as being used for document storage. Goodge Street served as an army transit camp until its closure was hastened by a serious fire in the mid-1950s. At around the same time it was revealed that only the four south London shelters retained the option for conversion to railway use, and the scheme faded into history. In the 1980s, some of the premises were leased as secure archives, with that at Goodge Street being commissioned as 'The Eisenhower Centre' in June 1986. Late in the following decade, the wheel turned almost full circle, when a number of the former deep level shelters were acquired by LT in association with up-grading existing facilities on the Northern Line.

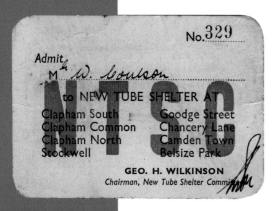

No. 329

Admit

Mᵉ W. Coulson

to NEW TUBE SHELTER AT

Clapham South   Goodge Street
Clapham Common   Chancery Lane
Clapham North   Camden Town
Stockwell   Belsize Park

GEO. H. WILKINSON
Chairman, New Tube Shelter Committee

This Pass is for use by persons requiring to enter the shelters in the course of their duty and does not authorise the holder to occupy a bunk in the shelter.

Signature of Holder   W. Coulson

(C46250)

The Tower Subway

This 2ft 6in gauge line stretched for a length of just 1,340 ft, but earned its place in history by being the first railway to be constructed within a 'tube' tunnel.

It linked the two banks of the Thames, and had its northern terminus at Tower Hill, close to the junction with Lower Thames Street. From its entrance, passengers descended by way of a 58ft deep liftshaft to a waiting room, from which they could join the car, or 'omnibus' as it was known. This vehicle was hauled by means of cables, which were attached to steam winding engines at either end, and completed its journey in one minute, ten seconds.

The station on the opposite bank was located on the west side of Vine Street, a short distance from Pickle Herring Street. This was 52ft below ground level, and had similar facilities to those at Tower Hill.

The car offered standard accommodation for all, although both First and Second Class tickets were issued. Of these, the former cost 2d whilst the latter was 1d, but the only advantage in paying the extra was that the passenger would be given priority in the lifts in event of overcrowding.

Sadly, the operation of this pioneering little railway proved problematical, so it was only in use for around three months after its formal opening on 2nd August 1870. The car, lifts and associated apparatus were removed, and the track boarded over. Stairs were installed in the former liftshafts, and on Christmas Eve 1870, the erstwhile railway re-opened as a foot tunnel. In this form it survived until being rendered redundant by the opening of Tower Bridge on 30th June 1894, and was soon taken over by the London Hydraulic Power Company which used it to accommodate pipework.

A contemporary engraving, published on 9th April 1870, showing the interior of a station waiting room, soon after the line was brought into experimental use, but before its official opening. Tickets were purchased at the street level kiosk, and appear to have been checked after leaving the lift.

Perhaps not surprisingly considering their early demise, photographs of the station entrances seem to be non-existant. This is a line engraving showing Tower Hill in 1870.

A new subway entrance opened on Tower Hill in 1871, and was rebuilt in 1926. This is how it appears today.

The car was 10ft long, and ran on four 16in diameter wheels. It had a height of 5ft 6ins, width of 5ft, and a space between seats of just 2ft 2ins, although this 1870 engraving makes it look roomier. It was clad in steel plating, and as it remained in tunnel, no windows were provided.

The Crystal Palace Pneumatic Tube Railway

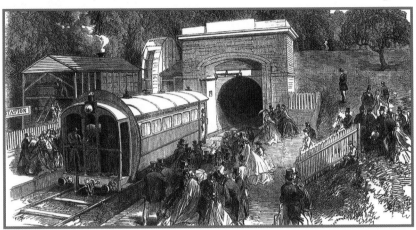

Rammell's carriage was built in Manchester and was described at the time as being *"very long, roomy and comfortable"*. It is seen here preparing to depart from the 'Sydenham Gate' station, with passengers joining on the left. Behind them stands the engine house, which utilised an adapted locomotive, mounted on a brick base, to power the fan. The tunnel was constructed largely above ground, so the hill behind its mouth was presumably added for artistic effect. The railway last operated on 31st October 1864 and, having served its purpose, was dismantled.

In the mid-19th century the engineer, Thomas Webster Rammell, was actively developing a means to operate railways by using pneumatic propulsion. His chosen method was to enclose a vehicle within a tube and use a large fan to either blow or suck it along the rails depending on direction of travel.

After a successful public experiment at Battersea in 1861 and the construction of a line to carry mailbags between the post offices at Euston and Holborn, Rammell thought it was time to utilise his system for transporting passengers. He hit upon the idea of building a pneumatically operated tube line beneath the Thames to link Waterloo with Whitehall, but before this could be done he needed to prove that his scheme would be viable.

In 1864 he built a demonstration line in the grounds of the Crystal Palace, which stretched for a little under 600 yards, with termini near the Sydenham and Penge Gates. It was only intended as a temporary affair, although illustrations of the 'Sydenham Gate' station show that the adjoining tunnel mouth was substantially built of brick.

The tunnel itself is thought to have been around 9ft wide and 10ft high, of which only 4ft or so was actually below ground level.

Passengers joined at 'Sydenham Gate' and for 6d could take a return trip to the Armoury near the Penge Gate. To demonstrate the practicality of his system, Rammell included curves and steep gradients, with the latter following the contours of the Palace grounds.

The line, which operated for just two months from August until October 1864, was seemingly a popular attraction with visitors and proved that Rammell's system was indeed suitable for carrying passengers. His Bill for the Waterloo & Whitehall Railway passed through Parliament unopposed in July 1865, but although some constructional work was carried out, the Company met with financial difficulties the following year, so Rammell's ambitious scheme for a pneumatic tube railway beneath the Thames failed to materialise.

An announcement which appeared in T*he Railway News & Joint Stock Journal* of Saturday 29th October 1864 stating that the *"Greatest Railway novelty of the day"* was about to close.

CRYSTAL PALACE.—LAST DAY OF PNEUMATIC RAILWAY TUBE, Monday next.—Greatest Railway novelty of the day.
Passengers conveyed through the Tube this day from One till Five. Return journey Sixpence.
Visitors in Carriages should drive to the Sydenham Entrance.

The Kingsway Tram Subway

The first section of the Kingsway Subway opened to public traffic on 24th February 1906, with a service of trams operating between the Angel and a subterranean terminus at Aldwych. It was intended to extend southwards to the Embankment, where connections would be made with other routes, but these had yet to be completed, so for a while the tracks beyond Aldwych were used as a depot.

Trams using the subway turned left at the west end of Theobalds Road, then descended a 1 in 10 ramp in the middle of Southampton Row. Once at the bottom they passed beneath the Holborn branch of the Fleet Sewer then, after a short climb, reached the intermediate station at Holborn.

A further station was authorised at Wellington Street, south of the Strand, but this would only have been around 200 yds from the Embankment and in 1907 was abandoned in the interest of costs .

Once the main Embankment routes had been brought into use, the subway link from Aldwych could be completed and from 10th April 1908 through trams began connecting Highbury with both Tower Bridge and Kennington Gate.

Initially the subway was served by a special class of single-deck clerestory roof cars, but as traffic grew it was decided to enlarge the subway so that it would take double-deckers. The last passenger-carrying single-deck car passed through on the morning of 3rd February 1930, then the tunnel was closed for rebuilding.

It was hoped that the work would have been completed by the end of the year, but it took longer than expected and the formal reopening did not take place until 14th January 1931. Six years later, the rebuilding of Waterloo Bridge resulted in the subway tracks being diverted slightly at their southern end to serve a new entrance. The changeover took place on 21st November 1937 and the short abandoned section of tunnel was walled-off.

In 1939 it was decided to explore the possibility of converting the subway for trolleybus use, but although a vehicle was provided with an offside platform so that it could serve the two stations, the scheme was abandoned.

The Kingsway Subway, with its stations at Holborn and Aldwych continued operating until the final year of the old London tramway system, but closed after traffic on Saturday 5th April 1952.

A southbound E/3 class tram working route 35 pauses at Holborn station on 8th March 1952, less than a month before closure. The roundels on the trackside walls were placed at two levels so that they could be seen by passengers travelling on both the upper and lower decks.

Aldwych station was similar in design to Holborn and is seen here, looking north on 30th March 1952. Aldwych station was demolished when part of the subway was rebuilt as the Strand Underpass, leaving little to indicate where it was once located. The Underpass opened to road traffic on 21st January 1964.

The northern section of the Subway, including the 1 in 10 ramp in Southampton Row, remains disused and is seen here in 1980.

The railings surrounding the former entrance to Holborn station were removed some years ago, but the stairways which led to the platform survive. Down below, the old station retains its tiled walls and shows evidence of where its roundels were once located.